CLIMBING MAYODAN MOUNTAIN

The People Who Could

by
Dr. Charles D. Killian

Published by:
Empire Publishing, Inc.
3130 US Highway 220
Madison, NC 27025-8306
Phone: 336-548-2735 • Fax: 336-427-7372
Email: info@empirepublishinginc.com

Climbing Mayodan Mountain: The People Who Could copyright © 2006 by Dr. Charles D. Killian

All rights reserved under International and Pan American copyright convention. No part of this book may be reproduced in any manner whatsoever without written permission from the author, except in the case of brief quotations embodied in reviews and articles.

Library of Congress Control Number: 2006926671
ISBN Number: 978-0944019-48-1

Published and printed in the United States of America

Cover Photo: Connie Fox

First Printing: 2006
Second Printing: 2013
1 2 3 4 5 6 7 8 9

With Gratitude

*to a wonderful congregation of United Methodists
who gave me a place to serve
four of the best years of my life;*

*to a small town that accepted me and made me feel
as one of 'its own';*

*to my wife, Jane, who has always made the journey
of 'climbing mountains' together
more pleasurable and exciting.*

Foreword

I grew up in Northern Indiana among storytellers. The seeds sown long ago in the soil of my life created in me a fondness for the anecdote, a thirst for stories and a fascination for how they were told and received. The narrative journey that began over 60 years ago took me into theological education. Even though I had an early heart-hunger for pastoral ministry, for the past 36 years I have taught preaching and storytelling at Asbury Theological Seminary in Wilmore, Kentucky.

Four years ago, the journey (some 40 years delayed) brought me to the pastorate, where I had thought to be all my life. In some way, I had about 40 years of preparation for one of my greatest assignments. Having been appointed to the Mayodan United Methodist Church, located in the Piedmont area of North Carolina, Jane and I found ourselves living, literally, in the shadow of Mayodan Mountain. For all the Providences of God that presided over this incredible pilgrimage, we will be forever grateful.

One of the first childhood stories I remember was "The Little Engine That Could." In brief, a long train must be pulled over a steep mountain but has trouble finding a willing engine because the job is too hard. The "Little Engine", with a courageous heart and a spirit of optimism, volunteers for the job, and you know the rest of the story… "I thought I could…"

For Mayodan United Methodists, "mountain" is a powerful symbol. Tornadoes, on two occasions, have destroyed the church, the most recently in 1998. Having survived, the dauntless and daring members have climbed their "mountain". Rising up out of the rubble, the church has emerged stronger and more determined than ever—assured that it can outlast any storm or turbulence that might come.

This collection of ramblings from my journal is intended to give you just a glimpse of the heart of this pastor and the indomitable spirit and character of this community of believers—a church that "could".

June 1, 2003

Front Porch Listening

This week afforded me two wonderful opportunities to develop the art of listening.

A Monday visit with Gertrude James

I had heard that she wasn't feeling well so I stopped by for a visit. What a trip! When you are with Gertrude, you listen. And if you listen carefully you can hear the meanderings of a gifted storyteller. She takes you down yesterday's roads and shows you sights and causes you to hear the sounds of her journey. She carried me back in her memory to her earlier years, her work at the mill, her time at Hardee's and at the Dillard School, finally retiring (for the second time) at the age of 72. Before she started her talking, she told me to take a seat as she hobbled over to the lamps and turned on the lights at each end of the couch. "Why did you turn on both lights, Gertrude? That wasn't necessary." She promptly replied, "I like to see the person I am talking to, even though I know you are the preacher." That felt warm and inviting—to be looked at is to be cherished.

I noticed her open Bible on the coffee table. She said the print is too small for her to read but gave me permission to leaf through it. I came across several napkins, many 50th wedding anniversary ones, and there was a story behind each one. She told me her favorite passages were in the New Testament and all those Jesus stories. So I read her the passage from last week's sermon from John 3, the story about Nicodemus. While I was reading it, she was constantly nodding, sometimes whispering 'yes, yes.' I came to one part where she informed me that she probably underlined that verse; and she had. We prayed together. She said she didn't have much strength to anymore but assured me she would pray for her preacher and her church. That felt warm and inviting, too.

We both went to the front porch and got comfortable in a couple of old iron rockers. There was a breeze coming around the corner of the house. She said, "If there is a breeze, it comes right around that corner." One hates to leave a breeze like that but it was time to go. "Gertrude, it has been a delight to spend some time with you today." And indeed it was: unhurried and full. She closed our communion together with another of her one-liners: "Preacher, I is what I is, and I ain't no isn't." I think I knew what she meant. It was 'vintage Gertrude'. Then I pulled away and we waved goodbye. I am glad I felt the 'gentle breeze' of being in the presence of that warm and inviting storyteller—one who 'is what she is.'

So I have been thanking God all week for that Monday session in LISTENING!

A Tuesday conversation with Ray Baughn

I met Ray on a couple of occasions and told him that one day I was going to stop and have him tell me some of his baseball stories. When I drove by his house he was sitting on the porch, waiting for me to stop by as I promised. Mayodan is a baseball town. Back in the 20's semi-professional baseball was being played here. Names of fame played in Mayodan; the likes of Paul Rizzuto, Enos Slaughter, Dominique DiMaggio to name a few. All of this piqued my interested as I asked Ray to share with me some of his stories. And off he went for over an hour. "When I was a boy about ten, I used to watch baseball here in Mayodan, but the only way I could get in (we had no money), was to fetch a ball over the fence back to the gate and that would get me in free. I feel in love with baseball. When I was fifteen, I was playing first base and I could stretch out there and catch anything that was thrown in my direction. That caught the attention of a scout who signed me for $15 a week. That began my ten years with baseball. Mayodan. Raleigh. Portsmouth. Burlington. Tallahassee. Even Odgen, Utah. By that time I was making $450 a month and that was some money when you didn't have any. I remember a home run I hit in Ogden. Out there in centerfield there was a scoreboard some 470 feet away. I came to bat in the bottom of the ninth and hit a ball over that scoreboard. Everybody was yelling and screaming. When I rounded the bases I was told that no one, nobody, had ever hit a ball over the scoreboard except Babe Ruth." We both grew silent. For a moment I was reverently silent. I thought—Ray Baughn is in the record book out there in Odgen somewhere, joining the Great Bambino, the Sultan of Swat, as the only two up until that time who had hit homers over the scoreboard in Odgen, Utah. We talked about his climb to Triple A in Rochester, New York. He talked unceasingly about his manager of World Series fame—Burleigh Grimes. He played against Yogi Berra. He even saw the great Lou Gehrig play. He told stories and I listened. Then he grew silent. "You know I might have made it to the 'bigs' if I hadn't been such a hothead. They wanted to send me to Atlanta and I said, 'No'. I walked away, simply walked away from baseball. I didn't want to go South, so I went back home to Mayodan. As far as I know I am still under contract with the St. Louis Cardinals,"

Now, some sixty years later, Ray has been waiting; maybe waiting for me or for someone to stop by and ask him about baseball. I felt he seemed a little saddened by walking away from baseball the way he did, but on the other hand, pleased, too, that he never did get a pink slip from the Cardinal organization. "When they released you, you got a pink slip. That meant you were done. Released. I never did get a pink slip." Ray chucked at that. But I also noticed a twinkle in his eye and heard him say with a labored voice that struggled with a 'lump in the throat,' "…as far as I know I am still a St. Louis Cardinal."

Many years ago, I, too, dreamed of the 'bigs.' Many were the days when I would wear myself out throwing and catching, batting small stones with an old 2 X 4, working the caroms off the barn that stood at the corner of our lot. I recall with vivid detail the lone new baseball that sat in the window at the LaMunion Hardware. $2.25. "Don't sell that baseball, Mr. LaMunion. I should have the money soon." I felt that it was the last baseball to be had in the world and I wanted it so. I was the happiest boy in all of Tyner the day I plunked down my $2.25 and got my first new baseball. I would throw it into the air and stare it like I was out there in left at Wrigley Field. Dreaming, always dreaming about baseball.

I cried the day that baseball got its first smudge—as if I had abused a small baby. Then came the scuff marks. After awhile the seams grew weary and began to unravel. It got stitched more than once. Finally, after many dreams and many miles of adventures, the ball lost its cover. The boy still dreamed.

The boy is still dreaming....and it was all faintly remembered again, sitting on Ray Baughn's front porch. Listening.

Don't be surprised by what you will hear and experience if you take time to listen.

God has been trying to tell me something, but for the life of me I have been so busy talking and doing stuff that He can't get a word in edgewise; that is, until Gertrude and Ray came along.

June 22, 2003

Flowers at the Side of the Road

I learned a new word today: 'sideoftheroadia.' If you say it real fast it sounds impressive. Tommy Martin helps us with flowers for worship. He does a good job. Normally, individuals support the flower ministry by giving resources in honoring or in memory of someone. Today we had no donors; so Tommy picked some greenery and hydrangeas from his yard and brought them to church early this morning. He needed something more so he went out to some country roads and picked some wild flowers. And when the arrangement was finished it would match anything we have had recently. He called the wild flowers 'sideoftheroadia'.

Who would have thought it—out there alongside the road are wild flowers gracing the roadside; waiting to bless those who see their beauty and can harness their extravaganza into a bouquet.

The metaphor or analogy is clear to me. Most of us are wild flowers out there alongside the road, often taken for granted, overlooked and undervalued. But along comes someone who sees something of exquisite beauty. And by some strange quirk of providence we find ourselves in 'the Master's Bouquet' adorning and blessing all who will but look. I looked out over the congregation this morning following my sermon and said the strangest thing. "We here at Mayodan United Methodist Church are a wild and strange lot of people…the kind of people that God is making into a masterpiece of His Grace. He is getting us ready for the next level of ministry in this place…"

Well, we are His strange and beautiful bouquet. And it seems that the more we worship together and get together the better we like who we are. The more we worship together the more like Christ we want to become. Right? Have you seen that commercial? You might have thought they were talking about Sunday worship. Here are some lines…Lets see if you can guess the commercial.
　"On Sunday morning, we look forward to…"
　"It gives me really what I want to know…"
　"It gives me a jump start on the week…"
　"I want to sign up…"
　"It is what Sundays were made for…"
　"There are parts of it I just don't want to be without…"
　　The New York Times.
It seems as if they have stolen our language and our conviction! What do we have to do to have folks saying that about worship?

Well, here at Mayodan, out here 'by the side of the road' we are attempting to become Christ's Presence in our community.

11

Worship is the key to all that we do...and I think it is what Sundays were made for—not for the *New Tork Times* but for the living in these times; even here among the wild flowers by the side of the road God is choosing to build His Church with the 'whole wild lot of us'.

July 14, 2003

After a Week Away

Jane and I just returned from a delightful week of vacationing at Oak Island with some 40 of our relatives. Early morning walks along the beach were invigorating. When you talk to God with no one around you get the feeling you've got His undivided attention. And then the crowd gathered, and the din and the chaos became a challenge to decipher amidst the creativity going on and the abusive intrusion of noise. Could it be age?

When I looked around and saw the newer generation (now twice removed) coming on the scene, there was no doubt I was watching a new paradigm developing by which to gauge what the newer generation will look like once we are gone.

Until then, do you remember...?
   Drinking water from garden hoses and not from a bottle? Horrors.
   Riding in the back of a pickup on a warm day? It was always a treat.
   When there were no childproof lids on medicine?
   When we rode our bikes without helmets?
   When we would leave home in the morning and play all day, until we heard Mother's call from the cellar door?
   Riding bikes or walking to a friend's home and knocking on the door, or just walking in and talking to them? Imagine such a thing.
   When you played games with sticks and stones?

> That before Little League, we had to choose our own teams and settle our own disputes without adult guidance or interference?
>
> Our actions were our own and consequences were expected?

I remember the day I broke out Charlie Calvert's garage window with an apple. He called the 'law'. I hid under my bed. Daddy called me downstairs and there in our living room was the biggest man I ever saw—a State Trooper with a loaded gun in his holster and dressed in blue ready to throw the book at me. I confessed to the crime. I thought surely I was headed to jail. Dad stood on the side of the law, and the two of them suggested that I apologize to Mr. Calvert and see that his window got repaired. After an apology and three weeks of allowances, the window was back in place. Mr. Calvert and I never did become bosom friends, but I learned some respect for him that day—that I was accountable for my actions.

I am not sure where all of this came from, given the ingredients in my vacation. When I returned to Mayodan, it felt like home. Within thirty minutes the phone started ringing and I knew the vacation was over. A myriad of tasks were awaiting my return like unanswered mail demanding a response. Yet, it <u>still felt like home</u>.

Why, just today, I saw Franklin Griffin. He told me that five years ago today, his wife, Shelby died. So Frank and I had lunch together. I got him to tell me how they met at the mill, how she got him up every morning and fixed breakfast, packed his lunch pail and had supper ready when he got home. She kept the checkbook, 'down to the penny.' She kept the house in order. They led a quiet, gentle life together. He said, "She was a Christian woman," and he reckoned that was why he was still going to church. Having lunch with Franklin bordered on being sacramental. He still misses Shelby after these five years; <u>talks to her every</u>day, he said. I asked him if he ever told her about the new preacher in town. "Oh yeah...oh yeah, yes." I thanked Franklin for the memory he had told me of his good wife. He made me feel more 'at home'.

Maybe it is my age. I keep seeing sermons all around me. I can't help feeling that I have been graced—by a family of forty wonderfully strange and beautiful people, and by a congregation that calls for the 'deep within me' to listen, to love, and to laugh.
I got to meet Shelby today...IT IS GOOD TO BE HOME!

July 20, 2003

It is All in a Week's Work

I really enjoy Sundays. Oh, there is the usual trauma of getting ready to preach on Sunday morning. I work on the sermon during the week, casting and recasting it in what I hope is the best possible way to present it. I get up early, get to the church a little before dawn, and work on it some more; even do a little practice on it. This morning when I woke up my immediate thought was: 'in a couple of hours I have a dental appointment'—thinking it was Monday morning, not Sunday morning. (I have an appointment with the dentist in the morning). Then I had the sobering thought, "What happened to Sunday? Oh, no, it is Sunday." I was a tad frantic as I struggled to make the mental shift. Then, I wondered—what would it be like not to have the Sunday obligation of preaching? What would I miss if I didn't have Sundays and all the wonderful people and the incredible experiences that go with it?

Monday—Rubee Sechrist came home from an assisted living center. With a change in her medical regimen and some physical therapy, her physical strength and mental well-being returned. What a joy to see the look in her face, delighted to be back where she most loves...home.

Tuesday—George Goad has returned home, too, after having had successful triple bypass surgery. You get the feeling it is not going to slow George down too much. He is 'chomping at the bit' to get back at chopping wood. It is amazing to watch the healing grace of God.

Wednesday—I meet with a group of ministers who discuss the Scripture lesson for Sunday. It was from Mark's Gospel, where Jesus, after an exhausting work schedule, instructed the disciples to 'get away from it all' and get some rest. We seemed to agree that a critical tension for us preachers is our always needing to be needed! Work, work, work….struggle, sweat, scheme. Most of us find it difficult to find that rhythm between work to be done and quiet restful recreation. I left that gathering, confessing that it was a most helpful discussion.

Thursday—I got a call from one of those telemarketers who wanted our church to sign up for the internet yellow pages. The salesperson said that the Mayodan United Methodist Church will appear on at least six web pages so that all those who are surfing the net to find out what resources the Mayodan United Methodist Church has to offer will be able to access it. I told him that I had about a hundred people who were much better than web pages—people who were let loose every Sunday about noon to get on with the business of being Christ's disciples in the Mayodan region. He was calling from somewhere in Iowa and I invited him to church, but we both agreed it would be too long of a commute.

Friday—Eddie Amos and I had lunch together today! I love Eddie. He is so honest and open with me. He loves his family. He loves his church, I have not met a more affirming person. As we ate together and fellowshipped at the Golden Dragon, I knew I was in the presence of greatness. I think Jesus would have agreed with me.

Saturday—Normally, Jane and I meet Ricky and Libby for

breakfast. It has become not only a delightful and exciting habit, but an indispensable reservoir of laughter and joy. To be with friends over a meal is a holy thing, indeed!

Sunday—I never know what to expect. Preaching is like scaling a mountain. It is hard work to 'reach the top'; and once you get there it is a sight to behold. You have the privilege to taking over a hundred people with you; then you have to let them 'go' for week and you are praying and trusting that what they saw and experienced was something of the risen Christ.

Jane and I topped our evening off with the Brantly and Cora Atkins family gathering. In one of the Sunday School Classrooms there is a piece of furniture that once graced their home but the greatest legacy that Brantly and Cora gave us was some incredible children, grandchildren, and great grandchildren.

Maybe it doesn't take much to excite me; maybe some would find my week rather routine and dull; maybe some would find it hard to stay on task with the day-in, day-out of my week's work…but I wouldn't exchange it for anything.

Well, tomorrow morning I will make my way to the dentist's office. I suppose if I look closely enough at that experience another sermon/story will leap out at me. In spite of my two times a day brushing and flossing, stuff still gets in the way and I need careful scrutiny from a professional dentist. I wonder—do the preacher and the dentist have anything in common?

Well, I kicked this memo off by asking 'what would I miss if I didn't have my Sunday obligation?' If I had to go from Saturday to Monday without a Sunday, I would have nothing, nothing at all.

August 3, 2003

A Child Can Say the Most Interesting Things

For the past week Jane and I have been in Wilmore, returning to fulfill my obligations in teaching. Tomorrow I start another class, finishing on Friday and returning on Saturday to Mayodan. But this morning in church a child said a most interesting thing. Let me tell you about it.

Jane and I worshipped at the First United Methodist Church in Lexington, a church where we have been associated for the past 20 years. I served as Assistant Pastor for two years and grew to love the people dearly. Pastor Al Gwinn asked me to be liturgist this morning for both services. I was thrilled and honored by this opportunity to assist in the worship. It was Communion Sunday. The people came forward to receive the bread and the cup. I noticed a little girl, hardly five years old, kneeling there beside her mother. When I came to her and offered the sacrament, I said to her, "Jesus permitted the little children to come to him, for to such belongs the Kingdom of God." She couldn't take her eyes off me. She chewed the bread and drank the cup, all the time looking at me as I continued serving others. After the service, her mother came to me and said, "I've got to tell you what my daughter said to me after we were seated." I was curious. Apparently, when they returned to their seats, the daughter was still gazing at me. She was having difficulty getting a good look, so she wiggled around and finally stood on the pew and said to her mother, "I can't see Jesus very well." We laughed. A child can say the most interesting things, can they not?

I have been thinking about that all day. "I can't see Jesus Christ very well." Here was one of 'the little ones'—in her childlike faith looking up at the preacher dressed in a black robe and white stole—kneeling with her mother, and the way she was looking at me indicated that this must be something very serious and somber. For her it must have been a 'Jesus Moment'. Naïve, sure. Mistaken identity, of course. A childish understanding, she'll get over it. On the other hand, for one brief moment she touched something deep. The 'deep something' was in me. The Bible talks about 'putting on the Lord Jesus Christ' as if He were our apparel. The Scripture is crystal clear about disciples being the 'image of Christ' in the world. It also speaks about the Church as the 'express revelation of Christ.' I don't know how many sermons I have heard over the years that spoke about our lives being the 'living expression of Christ.' In other words, is my life so lived that others see Christ in me? Maybe, just maybe, the little girl wasn't too far off base, after all. Let the truth of the gospel song ring deep within us all: "Let The Beauty Of Jesus Be Seen In Me".

August 11, 2003

What on Earth am I Here for?

This past Saturday I launched a new Sunday School class. The class wanted a discussion type class and we zeroed in on Rick Warren's best seller, *The Purpose Driven Life*.

There were 25 people who showed up for the class (about half of the regular Sunday School attendance) in crowded quarters. More books had to be ordered and it looks like we will be looking for new 'digs' in which to meet. What has been fascinating to me is the sub-title of the book, written right there on the bottom of the jacket cover: "What on Earth am I Here for?" Rick Warren has discovered in his work at Saddleback that this question is a landmark question for many. People are confused, disenfranchised, depressed and lonely—and they wonder: What is it all about; more to the point, what am I here for? The book addresses that quandary.

I thought I would help myself out a little before reading too far into the book; so I searched the internet, simply putting the question into my Google search engine. Aren't you delighted how handy it is to go to the internet for sources and solutions? Right there in front of you is the research, simply for the taking. Just maybe my electronic guru will grind out all I need to know to answer my query: What on earth am I here for?

Do you know what I discovered? There are over 1,253,000 responses to my question. It would take me almost a lifetime to go through that morass of information. I didn't get very far into that search until I had a more profound question. "What in the name of good sense am I doing?" I soon realized that if I had waded through all that material I would have died in the process and would still be left with the question unanswered.

Wonder why it is such a universal concern? Could psychologist Karl Menninger be right, asserting that "….the greatest mission field in the world is the inner emptiness of the human spirit"? When all the gadgetry and gimmickry have had their play, that is, when all the 'stuff' we have accumulated in hopes of making life more meaningful and pleasurable has had its day, millions will still pillow their heads at night bewildered and bemused. When the light dawns the next morning, THE QUESTION will come hauntingly and terrifyingly back with a vengeance. Because underneath all the clamor and chaos there is something to eat and something to drink that will assuage the agony that writhes in the pit of our gut. Interestingly, Warren begins his book with "It is not about you." The very first line serves as the thesis for what is to come. So there it is, right there in the beginning; he hits 'the agony that writhes in your gut' by stating you begin with GOD. He has a purpose for all His creation. If you trip up at that point, I suppose, the book will be a waste of time. Of course, you can read about 1,250,0000 responses if you want; or you can begin with GOD.

August 21, 2003

On Thursday

I never really feel like preaching until I have made some pastoral contact with my people. Maybe that's because I feel that James Cleland is right: "The preacher who is invisible six days a week will be incomprehensible on the seventh." That statement nags at me when the press of things crowds out that aspect of pastoral ministry. I knew I had to do it today. It has been awhile since I have made the 'rounds' to the various nursing homes where a dozen of our members reside.

I felt an urge to visit Beulah Woods. She is not a member, but I had heard she was in the nursing home so I made my way to Eden. When I arrived I learned she had died three hours prior to my arrival. I met Beulah a few months ago when I helped deliver 'Meals on Wheels' to her home. Don Stilwell and I took the meal in to her and Don introduced me and said, "Beulah is a prayer-warrior. She has a prayer list of over 500 names she prays for each day." I noticed the notebook, opened, there on her lap. She apparently had been praying when we entered. I was told she had cancer and was not at all well. Don introduced her to me as 'his preacher' and she smiled and said, "So you are the new minister at Mayodan United Methodist Church? I have been praying for your church." She showed me her prayer list. And I asked if I could be included. She beamed with delight. "Why, of course. That would please me very much." She turned the page and located a blank space and said, 'Sign-in.' My name joined a host of others. I told her that her praying for me meant a great deal. We had to hurry on to deliver the remainder of our meals, so we exchanged pleasantries, and with a brief blessing we were on our way. We got to the car and I told Don that we just received an enormous gift. To be prayed for daily means you'll never travel alone!

A few weeks later, I learned she was in the hospital and it didn't look good. When I entered her room, I saw the shell of a woman. Radiation and chemo had taken her hair and she had a scarlet head covering—but her face showed no signs of pain or dismay. She looked at me and said, "I knew you would come. I have been waiting for you. It is so good to see you." I acknowledged that it was her prayers that urged me to come. She smiled. After a brief word of Scripture, I had my last prayer with her. She did come home for a while but then was sent back to the hospital. Yesterday, I heard she was in a coma. This morning, no more coma.

As I left the nursing home, my childlike imagination envisioned her taking her 'prayer list' along with her, and when asked, "What trophies do you have to place at Jesus' feet?" she hands it to an angel (who doesn't have the foggiest notion of what she is talking about) who looks through that notebook, notices the tear-stained pages with over 500 names inscribed, and inquires, "What is this all about?" "I am content to have you just place it at the Master's feet, that is all," Beulah responds. And the Master opens the pages. Reads the names. All 500 of them. He calls out "Charles Killian, you prayed for him?" "Yes, and if it would please you, dear Jesus, may I keep praying for him?" And Jesus smiled and said, "We'd better." And they both laughed so loudly that some of the angels surmised that what had just happened must have been something big. Yes, real big! And to think this happened on Thursday.

Then I journeyed over to see others at Britthaven. When I walked into Ruth Barksdale's room she had just returned from the beauty parlor there at the nursing home and she was comfortable in her bed. Ruth was more subdued this time, but still managed one of her infectious smiles and mustered a weak greeting. "Pastor Chuck here, Ruth. You look so beautiful. Your silver hair is all in place. You look gorgeous." She said, "You look gorgeous too, but not as good as Johnny." (Johnny, her husband, died several years ago.) We talked about the Mayodan Church. When we talk about the Mayodan United Methodist Church, she lights up. We talked about her working with the children, the Sunday

21

School and the music, Bible School, and the people that she can still remember. I did most of the talking and she just nodded and said, "Yes, I sure do love the children." Ruth was not very responsive. As I looked at her, struggling to stay awake, I felt somewhat cheated; that is, I never had the privilege of knowing her when she was in 'full bloom' with of all her capacities. Then, the idea struck me—why not sing a song for Ruth and let her go to sleep? I started singing, "What a fellowship, what a joy divine, leaning on the everlasting arm...." And to my utter surprise she started singing with me, without missing a word. Then we sang, "Holy, Holy, Holy, Lord God Almighty...." We finished the first verse and she continued to another verse. "Ruth," I said, "You are fantastic. Let's sing a Christmas song. Want to?" "Yes, I love those songs." And the two of us had a little Christmas celebration in the middle of August. Angels long ago sang the first carol with the heavenly hosts; but today, Thursday, in a small corner of Ruth's half room; another angel sang and I wish all heaven and earth could have heard it. After my parting prayer, I noticed Ruth had fallen asleep. Sleep well, angel. You deserve the rest. And to think this happened on Thursday.

September 7, 2003

"It's Okay to Be Sad"

Becky Adkins went through life almost unnoticed. She was humble, always gracious. She could muster up a smile even through the pain of a thousand hurts. Her husband died of cancer many years ago. Her brother's life was cut short by a tragic accident. Her good friend, David Cook, died a year ago today. And for the past year she has carried deeply the hurt of so many unanswered questions surrounding his death. She made arrangements a few weeks ago to have flowers put in the church in David's memory. They graced our sanctuary this morning. Alongside those flowers was another basket of flowers in memory of Becky.

We were all shocked to learn of her sudden death this past Friday. Becky, at fifty, leaves three grieving children: Crystal, Laura, and Jerry. Becky was our nursery worker and caregiver at church. She was always early, eagerly waiting for the children to come. How the children loved Becky! So this morning, at children's sermon time, they gathered at the front of the church to hear from Pastor Chuck. Little Stevie wasn't sure he wanted to be up front with the pastor; he wanted to be with Becky…they all did and so did I. So we talked about being sad—that is was all right to be sad. Sometimes we lose something and can't find it. That makes us sad. Sometimes friends move away and we may never see them again. And that makes us sad, too. Sometimes we have a pet; a cat, a dog, a goldfish. And they die. We feel sad at that. Sometimes one of our best friends dies. And we feel lonely and sad. "It is okay to be sad," I told them. A little boy then said, yet aloud for me to hear, "I don't want to be sad." He wanted Becky and so did I.

I told the children about sitting on the concrete porch with Grandma Geller when I was a little boy. We would look up into the stars at night. Sometimes we would pretend to count them. "I love the stars, Grandma." "Me too," she would reply. I had questions about the stars. "Grandma, are the stars always up there? Why can't we see them in the day time?" We need the darkness in order to see them. Darkness is always beautiful when you look at the stars." In the midst of our darkness, our sadness, there is a light that shines. Grandma was more right than she thought, I suppose. When you don't look UP, you can miss the beauty of the night.

I suppose, in one way or another, death challenges our resurrection theology. It is rather easy to put our 'pilgrim theory' on a back burner. There is still the sting of mystery with death. Loss has a way of lessening our grip on things. We are made to stand still, even for just a moment, and wonder. Sometimes worry. And if you stop off very long in the valley of wondering and worrying, you never get an honest look at the darkness. "Darkness is beautiful

Death

when you look up at the stars." Stargazers are what people of faith are all about. Well, we all know that Becky beat us to the end of the race. She has finished the course. A crown awaits. Maybe that's my problem. Not the crown, but the waiting. How many more star-filled nights must I endure before the morning breaks? How many more times will I have to tell little, crying children, "It is ok to be sad?"

"Jesus wept." For whatever reason, Jesus cried. And when he finally wiped the tears away with the back of his hand, He got around to saying, "I am the resurrection and the life, the one who believes in me shall never die…." I guess it was His way of saying, "It is okay to be sad" but don't forget to "look at the stars. It can really be beautiful at night." That is the case if we are pilgrims on a journey—on our way HOME.

September 21, 2003

Forgiveness

I preached this morning from Matthew 18:21-35, the story of the "Unmerciful Servant." You know, the one who had been forgiven a debt (some scholars believe the astronomical sum was in the neighborhood of 150,000 years of salary). He was in an unfixable fix. He pleaded for mercy. Well, really, all he wanted was an extension of time. Maybe he could work it out, he thought. "Just don't foreclose on me." Instead of giving him a little more time (which in effect was just about as ludicrous as the amount of the debt), the master canceled the whole debt. He was freed from the debt. An outlandish, extravagant gesture on the part of the master. Apparently, the servant didn't really hear what the master said. He assumed he was still under the debt load (Maybe the news was too good to be true). At any rate, as soon as he left the presence of this magnanimous gift, he noticed someone who owed him around $10. He grabbed him by the throat…well, they knew the story. What he does is a reflection of his distorted understanding of 'grace.' God doesn't take too kindly to an unforgiving spirit. So, the story ends with his being thrown to the tormentors until every penny was paid back; which, of course, meant he was doomed to darkness. I mean, how do you pay back a debt that is unpayable? The only solution to his dilemma was what he was given in the first place. And that, he spit back in the face of the Giver. Could it be that what we have here is a story about living out a life of 'forgiving-ness'? And when we see these merciful acts from day to day…they blend into the flow of the river of His Grace. And the Kingdom of God comes, at best, when the forgiven, forgive; when the graced are gracious; and when the accepted, accept.

A little boy was standing at the Washington Monument. He said to the security guard, "I want to buy it." "OK," said the officer wanting to have some fun with the child. "How much do you have?" He emptied his pockets and found one dollar and thirty-seven cents. "Here's $1.37," said the boy. "That's not enough," said the officer. "I knew you would say that," said the boy. The officer then said, "Let me tell you three things about this monument. First, the Washington Monument is not for sale. Second, even if it were for sale you couldn't afford it; no one could; it is priceless. And third, if you are an American citizen it already belongs to you."

The same could be said about forgiveness. It is not for sale. You cannot earn it or pay for it. It is priceless. But if you are a Christian, a follower of Christ, it already belongs to you.

Forgiven Pilgrims, may God grant us grace sufficient to live a life with a forgiving spirit. It is a dangerous thing to 'hoard God's forgiveness.' May the mercy of our Lord Jesus Christ continue to dwell with you abundantly! Have a good week—living and forgiving.

September 28, 2003

Brunswick Stew and the Kingdom of God

I never ate Brunswick stew until I came to North Carolina a year ago. I came from Kentucky Burgoo to North Carolina Brunswick Stew. This past Saturday the Mayodan United Methodist Church brewed up about 250 gallons of the stuff. The process began on Friday night about dark and lasted until noon on Saturday. What a sight! In all, there were about fifty different people involved in the event. I was particularly drawn to those who stirred the cauldrons. With Billy Barrow around you soon learn the art of handling the paddle. The stew master would bellow, "Hold the paddle upright and keep it moving." Then we would hear, "More fire, more fire." It wasn't long till the water and all its contents were in full boil.

I left for bed around 10 P.M. because I was on 4 A.M. detail. I went home but couldn't sleep, so I got up and returned around 3 A.M. I got there in time to see the stage in the process when the bones were released from the meat. At the right time, per stew master Billy's schedule, the rest of the contents were added—potatoes, limas, peas, corn, sauces. Lord knows what else. I don't know how many gallons of Brunswick Billy has been responsible for, but when he talks, the rest of us listen. The crowds were to gather in about two hours and the stew master was barking out orders in a manner that suggested the stew was a long way from being ready. About 9 A.M. it was all coming together—ready and on time!

Right at 9:30, the gathered 'saints of the order of Brunswick' were ready. I never saw a more efficient assembly line than what we had in the dipping, the packaging and labeling. By 11:30 it was all over: sold, delivered and cleaned up.

It was a memorable day. Brunswick Stew Day at the United Methodist Church. I have been wondering since then about Brunswick stew. Where did it all come from?

The story of Brunswick stew is apt to provoke controversy because no less than three states claim to have given birth to the dish. Brunswick, Georgia; Brunswick in North Carolina; and Brunswick County, Virginia. The Virginia setting was a political rally for Democratic Party candidate Andrew Jackson in 1828, near the Nottoway River. A Dr. Creed Haskins hosted the event. He asked his long time cook, Jimmy Matthews, to cook up a stew, an original concoction of squirrel meat, onions, stale bread, and seasonings. The event was a success, Jackson was elected and Brunswick County's name was latched onto, as stories of the stew's honest flavor and savory simplicity were carried to other counties by those who attended the famous meal. Today, Brunswick stew maintains its legendary status as a symbol of warmth, hearth and home. This 'ambrosia' has been the staple for church functions, local fundraisers, family reunions, and political rallies for over 100 years. While Brunswick stew carries the title of the "Ambrosia of the South," the recipes have varied. One die-hard traditionalist lamented that squirrel meat is almost never used anymore. "I say that any true American worth their salt should use squirrel in Brunswick stew. Are we too citified to hunt, kill, dress and cook small game? Too prissy to gut an animal and clean the hide? Shame on you, America." Well, I think he's gone a little too far. Yet, there are recipes that call for dried thyme leaves, bay leaves, parsley, cloves, dry mustard, okra, vinegar, Tabasco, shoe peg corn, Boston butt, fatback and artichoke hearts. In spite of the varied recipes and the nature of its origin, the making of the stew is the story.

1. I saw the master passing on the tradition to the younger generation. If the Mayodan United Methodist Church is still making stew 100 years from now, I get the feeling that it will have the 'touch and taste' of what was taught years before the making.
2. I experienced an incredible fellowship in the making of the stew. The young and the old, men and women, skilled and unskilled, old-timers and newcomers—they were all there. We laughed and we partied. We kept the fire going and the pots stirred as we whiled away the night. With first light we

had the feeling that the night had been worth it. The smell of the stew wafted away in four directions. Soon another contingency came, ready to do what it was going to take to get it all done expeditiously. As if on cue, everyone found his/her place and the merchandise was packaged and ready for sale.
3. I observed that we had a commodity that was worth the effort. I heard people say that our stew was the best around. Some drove miles to get a gallon of it. Not one quart was left unsold.

For whatever reason—word of mouth, the taste test, or past experience—the stew had a market and we were ready. BRUNSWICK STEW AND THE KINGDOM OF GOD…is that too much of a stretch? Probably, but let me put it this way….

What are we passing on to the next generation about Kingdom values?
We have a story, a heritage, a prized commodity that we can only keep if we give it away.
What is your commitment to the task of Kingdom living?
We are a 'gathered community' that finds comfort, solace, direction and function by being together as "one in the Spirit."
How are we involved in the community of faith?

We are involved in something more than marketing stew. We belong to the 'fellowship of the unashamed' and we follow Wesley's dictum: "Offer them Christ."

Someone said, "Brunswick stew maintains its legendary status as a symbol of warmth, hearth and home…if the aroma says welcome and the taste says delicious, then the bowl of hospitality in front of you was born in Virginia."

May the same be said of the church. "May the status of the Mayodan United Methodist Church always be one that welcomes all with our 'open hearts…open minds…open doors', a place to feel warmth and at-homeness; a place where the fragrance of the Spirit of Christ is manifested and lived-out."

October 13, 2003

Songs in the Night

It is early Monday morning and I feel good in my soul. I have heard that sometimes 'Mondays' can get you down. I wonder where that came from? Maybe after a great weekend away from the work-world responsibilities you come face to face with another world that is antithetical to the delightful joys that come with Friday and its weekend release. Well, on this particular Monday morning, I feel good in my soul…Why?

Last evening, Jane and I returned from visiting Daniel Tuggle, Cindy and Steve, and the Perdue family at Carolina's Medical Center in Charlotte. It was just 48 hours ago that the doctor told the family that unless surgery were performed immediately on Daniel he might not live an hour. The doctor said, "You must give Daniel to me right now. I will do my best to relieve the pressure on his brain. It is 'touch and go'. But I want you to go to prayer and pray for Daniel and me." It is the kind of news that 'rocks one to the core'. Daniel was placed into the hands of a skilled neurosurgeon and the Great Physician. People all over the country were praying for Daniel.

The word was that Daniel, if he should survive, would have a most difficult road ahead of him. The family was warned that he might not be able to open his eyes for some time, that his speech could be very slow in coming back, that rehab would be difficult, and that he might not recognize the family. The family faced the possibility of grim consequences with resolve. Following surgery, the doctors were pleased that all went well. Caution was advised.

Optimism was tempered with 'the next 48 hours are critical'.

Critical they were. Periodic reports indicated that there was a good heartbeat, some brain wave activity, and strong blood pressure. Shortly thereafter, Daniel was able to respond to some voice commands, like 'nod your head. Hold up two fingers'. When he did that, everyone was pleased. Sunday was greeted with more good news. Around 9:30, Daniel was elevated in his bed. He was talking. He wanted to know when he could go home. He was breathing on 'his own'. Many of the tubes were removed. When I walked into his intensive-care room about 5 P.M. last evening, with labored voice and half-shut eyes, he said, "Pastor Chuck." I, along with other members of the family, surrounded his bed with enormous delight, knowing that we were in the presence of a 'miracle'.

We had prayed together, thanking God and celebrating the 'life-flow' that was surging back into Daniel. When I finished, Daniel let out a reverberating "Amen." Amen, indeed! I asked Daniel what he would like to say to you all. He said, "Tell them all, hello."

Well, good morning and 'hello' to you all from Daniel and Pastor Chuck. Daniel does have a long way back. Do keep him and the family in your prayers. You know something…it is good to be placed in the 'hands of a skilled Physician'. It is good to be a part of a family of God that knows no Name, save Jesus Christ. It warmed my heart beyond description that I had a brother who lives near the hospital in Charlotte who was so available and supportive to the family until I could get there. It brings joy to the heart to be the pastor of a congregation that enters into the suffering of others so caringly and compassionately.

Job said it a long time ago, "Where is God who gives songs in the night?" An honest prayer. He lost his wife, his children and all his possessions. He was going through 'a night.' And he wondered. After his doubts and his questions, he could exclaim courageously, "I know that my Redeemer liveth." None of us are exempt from the tragic and traumatic. Yet, in the midst of it all there is a solid affirmation and a sound foundation on which to commit our 'nights'. God is in charge! That is what the doctor told the family the other night, during their 'night'. And morning has broken…a new day has come. We have been given 'songs in the night'.

October 19, 2003

Should the Red Sox Give Up?

I am a forlorn and saddened Boston Red Sox fan! It happened again this week. In the bottom of the 11th inning, the Yankees pulled it out, the Red Sox went down to defeat. I confess I am an avid Boston Red Sox fan. It goes back to when I was a kid. Ted Williams was my idol. I remember the day the Army called him into active duty and I wept. It took four years out of his baseball life, mine too!

In 1946, Boston lost the World Series in the seventh and final game. I was eight years old and my world was coming apart—Boston lost! It happened again; 1967, 1975, 1986. They lost the World Series, and they lost them all in the seventh and final game. In the 1986 series with the Mets, the Mets lost the first two games, then won two out of three at Fenway. Boston was leading in the sixth game but the Mets rallied to win, taking the series to a seventh game which the Mets won, rallying from behind to do it.

The poor Red Sox! In 1978, they were 14 games ahead, in first place going into the last weeks of the season, and lost the pennant on the last game of the season. You get the feeling that fate is against them. Boston fans are tormented by these facts. It appears that there is a chance about every 18 years, on the average, and they blow it every time, usually in the seventh game. So I raised the question: after 85 years of trying, should the Red Sox give up and concede that fate is against them? Is there some power that is controlling the destiny of things so that even our best efforts are not able to succeed? That '86 series still haunts me. Do you remember how they got into that series? They were playing the Angels for the title. They were trailing. It was the bottom of the ninth. Two outs. Dave Henderson comes to the plate. Two strikes in the bottom of the ninth. He wrote later: "We're ball players, and ball players fail most of the time. But I have got to do it. I have got to get the ball in there somewhere." And he did. I saw it happen. I was in the Atlanta Airport, on my way to catch a flight. I saw it on the TV. Henderson waits for the pitch. He hits a home run. It was the kind of victory that gave me hope that maybe this would be the year (1986) for Boston and a World Series ring. But no, it just wasn't to be! So you can imagine my heartbreak this past Thursday night. The Yankees win again and deprive the Red Sox of another chance. So, I ask it again—should the Red Sox just give up and throw in the towel?

Well, not in this kind of a world. Not in a world of possibility. Because the Red Sox problem was not on Mount Olympus (as if gods were against them). Rather, I suspect, it was in the bullpen and the Yankee mystique. The gods weren't against them, the odds were. And what that basically means is—you don't give up. Back in '86, following their loss, a reporter was interviewing Dwight Evans, one of Boston's best players who had learned a few things about baseball and about life, wondering if he could still hold his head up. Evans said, "I won't hold it up or down. I'll just keep looking straight ahead. That way if something good comes along I'll see it." (Thanks to Mark Trotter for this idea.)

That is what faith looks like. We depend not on our own efforts, but on God's grace. It means that you can lose the Series and still look for something good to come. Because next spring, the Red Sox will gather for another shot at it. Spring training. They will lace up their cleats and get themselves ready for another season—hopefully, looking for 'something good' to come.

I remember the large sign above the basketball scoreboard back home. It said, *"When the great scorer comes to write against your name, he writes not whether you won or lost—but how you played the game.*" I suspect the Red Sox will be thinking about that as they linger through the winter waiting the first call of spring and 'play ball.' But the larger issue is this: if baseball is a metaphor for life then it is not win or lose, but how you play the game. Jesus said as much, too. He said that the one who hears His words and abides in Him, is like the man who built his house upon the rock. And it stood in the midst of the rain and the floods. The foolish one built his house on the sand. And the rains and the floods came and that house was destroyed. You play this game on the 'rock' or on the 'sand.' One loses, one wins! It is up to you! How are you going to play the game?

That's why baseball is so full of mystery. It calls us to participate. To take sides. To dream. Your delight or your delusion last for just a season… Springtime is just around the corner and we all will go through the ritual again. Always looking for 'something good' to happen. That's why, too, this journey of faith is so full of mystery. It calls us to participate. To 'play the game of the Rock." Yes, we will go through a series of wins and losses. But we are determined to play, always looking for 'something good' to happen. GOOD always happens to those who are looking for it. Even for this 'forlorn and saddened' Boston Red Sox fan.

November 1, 2003

Baseball Story

Mayodan is a baseball town. A mill town. And it loves baseball! So I have another baseball story. Talking about baseball, I should be the happiest baseball fan around. The Boston Red Sox and the Chicago Cubs are in the playoffs. For some strange reason, the Boston Red Sox has always been my favorite team, and the Chicago Cubs was a close second, largely because I grew up 60 miles from Chicago. I rooted for both teams and many were the times when I thought my teams were going to 'do it,' only to be disappointed year after year.

I don't know if Abner Doubleday was a theologian. But he was a general in the army. And being a nineteenth century man, he possessed a strong Protestant 'work ethic,' which meant he was imbued with hard work and tenacity…the type of person who strives for perfection. But who can be perfect? Doubleday invented a game that dramatizes the predicament, a sort of morality play on the theme of justification by grace through faith and not in works. The game of baseball is a drama of attempting to live under a law of perfection and always falling short.

Baseball is a game of numbers. Every ball and strike is counted. Every 'at bat' is counted. RBI's, ERA's, batting averages, fielding percentages—everything is measured. What is more, everyday the current batting average is printed in the newspaper for the whole world to see. And the average is carried out to three decimal points. They don't say, "He hits pretty good." They say *precisely how* he is doing – "He hits .317, or .247." Nothing is overlooked in analyzing his performance. You can't fake it in baseball. Perfection is quantified in absolute terms, held up to a standard of perfection, and then put down in the book forever.

But the genius of the game is that it is built on grace, too. The game has 'grace' written all over it. Everybody gets three strikes and four balls. Everyone has an opportunity to bat. Everybody gets at least three opportunities to hit the ball. But the most gracious part of baseball is that it has no clock. It is about the only major team sport that is not governed by the sweep of time. The game goes on until everybody has had a fair chance of winning. Yogi said, "It is not over till it's over."

We laugh at that, but it is a significant theological statement. It is what grace means. It means you have another chance. Life doesn't erase your errors or your sins, but you are given a chance to live as if they weren't there. You're given a chance to live as if what happened in the past doesn't count. We always miss the mark. St. Paul writes about this. He said those who live under the law make an attempt at perfection but always fall short of it. The amazing thing about all of this is that nobody's record is very good. The point of going to the plate is to get a hit. That is what the player gets paid to do. The better players hardly succeed in doing what they get paid to do. About one-third of the time they get a hit. Think of what it would be like in your job if your performance record were like that. If, on a scale of 10, your performance record never got over 3, you'd get fired. In baseball, if you get a 3, you might get an extended contract and a raise.

When Mickey Mantle was reminiscing about his career, he recalled that he had struck out 1,210 times and walked 1,734 times. "Which meant," he said, "I was up to bat 3,444 times without ever hitting the ball. You figure a player playing regularly will get to bat about 500 times a year over a season. That means I played for 7 years without ever hitting the ball." Grace says you can strike out 1,700 times and still be a winner.

November 3, 2003

Look at This Man

This past weekend, Ricky and Libby Sechrist, Jane and I, flew to Tulsa and drove to Carl Junction, Missouri, where we met and worshipped with the United Methodist congregation whose sanctuary was destroyed by a tornado last May. On our flight into Tulsa, the pilot announced that riding on the plane was a soldier who was returning home from Iraq for two weeks of R&R before returning to Iraq. The entire cabin of passengers burst into spontaneous applause. He was a young man, early twenties. I had a brief chat with him. I expressed my appreciation for what he was doing, 'laying his life on the line' for the likes of us all. He used the word 'memorable' when I asked him what word he would use to describe his experience. He said the soldiers were, for the most part, accepted there and greatly valued, but "…during the night that is when it gets scary. The ugly element comes out when it gets dark…" I offered him the "Peace of Christ" and told him that I would be praying for him and all our troops. He said that he appreciated that very much. I watched him walk, all alone, down the airport corridor on the beginning of his two weeks of R&R, knowing that after an all-too-brief stay at home he will be back in Iraq, a torn place, "especially during the night, when it all gets scary."

We had a delightful time in Carl Junction, a small town, about the size of Mayodan/Madison combined. On Saturday night we viewed the ruins. Nothing but a slab remained where the church once was. Several had been in the church for choir practice. They saw the storm coming. They had no place to go but into the restrooms. In a few short minutes it was all over. When they emerged from their 'shelter in the time of storm' they discovered that their church lay in ruins. They were alive! They had reasons aplenty to rejoice! It is amazing how that little town has come together. You can read it on a big billboard coming to town: *"We Once Were Neighbors, But Now We Are Family!"* They are going to rebuild. Out of the ashes of destruction, they are emerging valiantly and courageously. We caught a glimpse of that in worship, where they gather each Sunday now (and will for at least a year) in a half-dozen mobile buildings serving as their worship center and Sunday School headquarters. It was good to hear Ricky and Libby give their witness. When they presented the banner that expressed our linkage to them, there was hardly a dry eye in the congregation. When we presented them with a check for $1,500, they were in awe that a small congregation, still struggling to come out of 'its own ashes' would come half way across the nation to offer support and encouragement. It was a good moment for us to be there. You know, the soldier was right…during the night, 'it gets scary'.

And we take comfort and strength, knowing there are others who are praying for us…who are walking alongside us. Carl Junction and Mayodan are joined together because we are a part of the family of God; because we share in a disaster; because we have experienced 'a scary night' together—and the space between our congregations will now and forever be sacred space.

We arrived home around 10 P.M. and a phone message indicated that Norris Griffin had been taken to the hospital. I called Anne and got the details and went to visit him this morning. Norris was sitting in a chair, talking to the head nurse. When I walked in, the nurse said, "Why, here comes someone to visit with you." Norris introduced me as his pastor. She said, "We have just been talking about Jesus." That intrigued me; so after getting caught up on his condition, I inquired about her comment. Norris said that the nurse was remarking to someone in the hall that this person's mother sure didn't look her age. The nurse said, "Why look at this man (pointing to Norris). Tell her your age." Norris said that he would be turning 85 real soon. They lady looked at Norris and said, "Do you go to church?" "All my life," Norris replied. Then she said, "I have observed that older people live longer, happier lives when they have grown up in the church." For those who know Norris, we want his life to be longer and happier, still! The nurse couldn't fully comprehend the impact of her statement on me when she said, "Now look at this man…" Yes, take a good look at Norris. He walks tall and confidently; yet humbly. He speaks quietly and soberly, yet clearly. He lives and loves Christ; confidently.

I suppose it gets 'scary at night' for Norris, too! Facing tomorrow resolutely, his faith is anchored in Christ—his 'shelter in the time of storm'!

November 23, 2003

At the End of the Perfect Day...Well, Almost!

Every once in a while you have one of those days that rivals the eating of fresh raspberries and cream. Every now and then you have a day that you don't want to end. Once in a blue moon you want to put a 'hold' on the day and relive it as often as you want.

Sometimes you are treated to a grace-filled day in such proportions that you don't have the foggiest as to what has happened. Well, really, the day got started yesterday. Jane and I were riding through Madison when Jane saw one of the 'messages from God'; you know, those one liners like, "What part of 'thou shalt not' don't you understand?" This one read: "Don't make me come down there." –God

Interesting! It is only one of those God statements that is false. God *did* come down here, not as an angry parent who might shout upstairs to some unruly children, "Don't make me come upstairs," but as a loving father who took the initiative to come to us in Christ in spite of our waywardness.

We are upon the Advent Season. It begins next Sunday. With anticipation we await the arrival of that 'invasion' from the Other World. And that has made all the difference.

So, when Jane pointed that message out to me, I laughed. I remembered Mama as the one who hollered those words upstairs to me on more than one occasion.

But upon more sober reflection, I guess I did make Him 'come down here' after all. My sinfulness and my meanness broke His heart because my heart, too, was fractured and broken. I reckon that realization does give a 'feel' to the possibility of a 'perfect day.'

Today, our church dedicated our Thanksgiving Sunday Offering for debt reduction. For reasons that are numerous and have little merit in my revisiting them at this time, the debt has been an albatross about out necks. It has been difficult to make budget. I have felt for some time that God would be pleased and honored if we could rid ourselves of this obligation. A year ago, we raised $20,000 and it was a shocker that we could do that in one offering. The Board decided to do the same this year. In a year in which the economy and the stock market have been in the pits, the thought of repeating last year's amount was dismissed by some as impossible. This morning, we all were 're-shocked' when the report came in: $28,117. We closed out the service, singing, "To God Be the Glory." Indeed. God did come down here! It just could be that this kind of 'God intervention' on our behalf is what the doctor ordered. A hefty belief in ourselves; a resolve to get done what needs to get done; and an unbridled trust in a God who let us in on one of His great secrets—"Unless He does come down here, there is little we can do."

Tonight we had our second Community Celebration Worship Service. Eighty-five were in attendance. It was a good time. A good spirit. Seventeen newcomers gave us a worship attendance for the day of 153. That hasn't happened in a long time. God keeps on 'coming down'.

Maybe I ought to write some God-statements; some one-liners. What about these?
    If you let me in the church, I will take over. –God
    You can't out -give Me, I have the bigger shovel. –God
    Trust me. Period. –God
    If you don't worry about who is going to get the credit, don't be surprised by what can be done. –God
    If I own 'the cattle on a thousand hills,' $28,117 is just peanuts. –God
    ….enough already!

It is Thanksgiving week. Whatever your plans, have a great

Holiday, safe travel. As I am about to pillow my head for the night, it comes to me that today, this day, this almost perfect day, could be the turning point in the life of the Mayodan United Methodist Church. Not because of the offering, not because of the spirited good worship both this morning and evening, and not because we are deserving...but because God in His infinite Wisdom, here and there, now and then, breaks through our cussedness and gives us a 'perfect day' because of who He is. The next time you see that sign: *Don't make me come down there! –GOD,* write your own message, like: *I came down there, so look out! –GOD.* Yes, at the end of this almost perfect day, "To God be the glory...great things he has done..."

December 1, 2003

Black Friday

BLACK FRIDAY—that is what they called last Friday, the day following Thanksgiving. It started about three years ago when merchants looked upon the day following Thanksgiving as the day to put them in the 'black'; that is in the profit position. Well, some of them did right well. Take Wal-Mart for instance; they did a billion and a half dollars for their operation. Quite impressive, don't you think? I drove home from my brother's home on Black Friday and as I made my way around the city of Charlotte, I could readily see that the traffic flow was almost coming to a stop. For a mile the traffic was backed up on the interstate, waiting to make exits to the malls, I presume. Hungry and desperate shoppers going for their prized possessions, awaiting them at Goody's, K-Mart, Belk's, and the like. And they were willing to clog up traffic only to get to the stores, only to find that long-awaited DVD player and the Barbie's were sold out. Can you imagine someone slugging it out over a Barbie Doll? That is what happens on Black Fridays.

Where did that term come from? Historically, it was first dubbed on September 24, 1896, when James Fisk and Jay Gould attempted to corner the gold market on Wall Street. It caused incredible panic. The markets fell. Some thought the world was coming to an end. It wasn't until the U.S. Government sold millions of ounces of gold that the market finally stabilized. Fisk and Gould netted nearly $11,000,000 for their shenanigans. That was the first Black Friday. The dictionary defines shenanigan as "a devious trick…a tricky practice…mischievous activity…" I understand that one of Webster's definitions of 'black' means 'show profit'. I guess the juxtaposition of 'showing a profit' on the heels of Thanksgiving seems a little awkward for me. We all know it is the inauguration of the Christmas shopping season. I am told that some merchants will either make it through the year or go 'belly up' based on their receipts on Black Friday. I guess more than anything it is the name 'Black Friday' that gives me pause.

So, I went to my computer, hit my MSN search engine for Black Friday and 2,482,144 entries were there waiting for me to explore all of its intrigue and mystery.

In many ways the 'blackest' of all Fridays is the one we call "Good." So I hit the MSN Search Engine for it and behold, there were 35 entries. That's right – 35. I am not going to make any theological statement about the difference, only to suggest the enormous fascination with the 'black side' of things.

Think of the many ways in which we use the word:
    Black ball…
    Black book…
    Black Death …
    Black eye…
    Black flag…
    Black out…
    Black sheet…
    Black market…
    Black magic…

Even Black heart… "a plant disease in which the central tissues blacken."

All of these 'blacks' carry negativity with them. Here we are, in the second day of the Season of Advent. The mad rush is on! Merchants are wanting a 'to be continued' Black Friday, of course. And in all of our shenanigans, too, the 'black side' of things gets perpetuated when we fail to notice that there are still some mad Herods around…that Rachel is still weeping for her children and cannot be comforted…and that the 'silent stars go by' unnoticed. On the other hand, could it be that is was our 'blackness of heart,' our 'dark night of despair' that God had in mind when the birthing of the Christ Child took place long ago—right in the middle of our 'black Fridays'? So journey with me: quietly, carefully, resolutely…knowing full well that Good Friday will have the last word.

December 5, 2003

Advent Plea for Slowing Down, but This?

Last Sunday, I urged us all to slow down and be less intense during the Advent Season. I even asked you all to pray for me that it would happen in my life. Well, let me tell you… Monday evening, I took ill and have been in the house ever since. Four days of salt water, drugs and some over the counter stuff. Things haven't improved much. It took a good week to shake it way back then with little more than cod liver oil and grandma's concoction of herbs that had to be inhaled for thirty minutes under the shroud of a blanket. This week, about $60 worth of cures that you thought would hasten the healing, but no, it is going to be another one of those 7-day deals, I fear.

Well, frankly, I kept faith with my meditations and prayers during the week. In spite of all that, with a headache and every bone aching, I would look out the window and note that there was plenty waiting to be done. One ought not to be so messianic.

I am hoping to go to Leroy Collins' funeral tomorrow. He was one of my 'members' at 'Ann's Chapel' (local coffee drinking pub). I am trusting I will be well enough to make worship on Sunday; so I am asking a favor: Please pray for me that God will quickly deliver me from this illness. It just seems to be hanging around longer than usual.

I am kinda like the lady who realized that she hadn't sent her Christmas cards out, so she went to a card shop and picked ones that had a nice Christmas motif on the cover, raced home and mailed them. Later, to her surprise, she read the printed message on the inside which read: "I am sending this card your way just to let you know that a small gift is coming your way in a few days." There are times I want to be so proper, so prepared, and so predictable that I am driven to struggle with an unsought-for and not-needed illness to remind me that I am not in charge. The outside looks fine and appropriate, but the message inside reveals so much. Make sure you read the inside of your life during this Season. Life is precious and fragile; each day counts. The Bible says, "…a small gift is coming your way in a few days." That is SO right! Let's not miss it.

December 29, 2003

Looking Both Ways

Sickness and the rush of the Season put me on the 'back burner' for my writing; so here goes again. I love the Christmas Season— the songs, the children, the colors, the pageants, the giving and receiving. It all reminds us of the fact that grace is still around. I saw 'grace' the other day. Maybe you did, too. Have you ever been asked by a panhandler for money to get something to eat or drink? If you don't plan to respond to them, make sure you don't make eye contact. He worked me for two quarters. "Thanks so much." Yeah, right! Down the sidewalk there was a man ringing the Salvation Army bell next to his kettle, somewhat out of the way of the foot traffic, so that it would not seem "too offensive to the shoppers," so he was told. While I was contemplating the scene, this elderly man, unkempt, poorly clad, dropped my two quarters into his kettle, saying only, "Coffee for somebody." His act of grace mocked my hollow generosity. He taught me a fresh lesson about 'grace', if nothing more than the fact that he knew something about the Salvation Army. How they brew uncalculated millions of cups of coffee in the midst of the direst of situations. He might have gotten himself a cup one day at a rescue center or at a corner in weather below freezing, without any questions asked. "Without Any Questions Asked"—I am sure it'll be title for a Christmas sermon next year. It will take me a year to recover from the awesome re-awakening of such a story-event. Grace is like that—'without any questions asked!'

We stand at this particular time of the year between two journeys: one taken, one to be taken. Looking back, looking ahead. But between the two is a more incredible journey—looking within! And we don't have much time to do it. 2003 is almost history, 2004 an uncharted sea. What are you going to do with it? Let me suggest one thing. Mr. Claude York was my history teacher and gave us some unbearable memory work. One day, around Christmas time he told us that during World War II, King George VI gave a broadcast to the Commonwealth of England. In one of his Christmas addresses, during the very dark time, the King included these lines,

> I said to the man who stood at the gate of the year,
>   'Give me a light that I may tread safely into the unknown.'
> And he said to me,
>   'Go out into the darkness and put your hand into the hand of God.
> That shall be to you, better than light and safer than a known way.'

Then Mr. York would bellow, "Memorize those lines. Don't ever forget them."

You can do that, you know. You can put your hand into the hand of God—without any questions asked. If you do, don't be surprised if here and there, now and then, you will hear, "Coffee for somebody."

January 25, 2004

Bliss

My brother, Bill, used the word, 'bliss' to describe what was going on in his life right now. Bill recently retired as chaplain at Tucson Medical Center. Along the way, he has performed in theatrical productions that have given him enormous delight, even had a part in the film, *Family Plan* (starring Leslie Nielson). Now retired, he has the luxury to give more time and attention to his craft. At the present time he is starring in the stage production, *Streetcar Named Desire*. He is in a state of 'bliss' he says. Good for Bill! He is one creative guy with loads of talent and drive. I was captured by that word. Been thinking about it for days. BLISS. The dictionary states that 'bliss' means: "state of complete happiness; almost paradise and heaven-like." What a way to describe the goings-on in ones life! A state of bliss!

Thanks to Bill, I am borrowing the word, too. After thirty-two years in academia, while at times 'blissful,' the word never entered my thinking until I came to Mayodan. I've been trying to put the right descriptive word on it, but nothing quite fit until Bill sent me the word via his own journal. We each, Bill and I, have our own performing stage. The stage on which pastoral life is performed has its own exits and entrances. We both play to the audience, as it were. There is also the agony of getting the production together and getting it right; and then when it is over, you move to the next venue. Our scripts are different, though, quite different. Why, just last week, while visiting with Ruth Barksdale, I found myself feeding her lunch. She said she liked spinach and chicken salad. For thirty minutes I fed her lunch, slowly. Ruth doesn't talk much now. She seems to be looking down the road. We prayed together and she said she loved me. A moment of bliss! Stopped by to see Ray Baughn who hopes to be out of the rehab nursing home by the end of the month. Ray is one of the oldest members of our church, but it has been decades since church has been a part of his life. When I got ready to leave he said, "When I get out of here, you and I have got some catching up to do." I knew what he meant. It was another moment of bliss for me!

I cannot describe the utter 'bliss' I had this past week, teaching seventeen students something about the art of preaching and storytelling. It all wound up with my getting caught again by the inexpressible joy in telling stories: our stories, His Story. Come to think of it, most of my life has been surrounded by stories, stories that got started back there in my early years. At Blissville Church of the Brethren. Yes, Blissville. I am recalling my first religious experience, there in Wilda Bottorff's Sunday School Class. I don't remember anything she said, except at our offering time. On the table in front of us were two banks, one a church, the other a globe. She said, "If you want to give your offering to our church, put it in the church bank; if you want to give it for missions, put it in the globe bank." I always gave my pennies to missions. I am not quite sure why, but that experience is etched on my memory…a memory that eventuated in action that has borne fruit around the world. And it all got started in Blissville!

When we Killian kids were small, mother took us to Blissville Church. On the way to church we played a game called, "I see the church." The first one to see the church, called out: "I see the church." Grandma and Grandpa Geller were there waiting for us; Wilda Bottorf, too. And that little globe mission bank. In my mind's eye, I can still see that church, water pump off to the right and the outside toilet in the back. Just thinking about it brings 'bliss' to my heart. Well, the story has almost come full circle. The script keeps changing. Audiences are still expecting me to show up. Venues? What is next? When the curtain falls on the final act, what then? The incredible drama that I have been involved in can't go on forever. Or can it? Bliss…utter Bliss. Until then, a little foretaste of what is to come greets me every morning—whether I am offering 'spinach and chicken salad' in Jesus Name or teaching a class in Moscow or telling a story, any story—it is all bliss! What word would you use to describe the journey you are on today? If you want, I can take you to Blissville. It could be right there in front of you!

February 2, 2004

Super Bowl or Sacred Bowl

32-29…you get the picture! For all of us Panther fans, it was not the finish we were hoping for…well, that is another story.

Yesterday was Sunday, the Sabbath! Hardly. It was Super Bowl Sunday. Football was 'king' yesterday the game of games! Super Bowl always sits on the throne, a godlike throne. The total professional football season is reduced to this one game to determine the world champion. You get the impression that the hype that went into the 'getting-ready' phase of the game took on the dimensions of eternity. The almightiest lined up on both sides of the scrimmage line and went at it. They bruised and banged at each other for sixty minutes to determine who was the mightiest diety of all. Multimillions of us were glued like paste to TV's across America and around the world. The sacred feast was carried to the Third World, along with those behind the Bamboo Curtain.

When one gets caught up in a ritual of this order and magnitude the message must be thorough. Gods of a lesser order demand it. People gathered around video receivers as if they were altars on which to offer allegiance. The witching hour came and the world stopped for a while. The coin was tossed and the worship hour was on! Pity the church with the other God begging for an audience. Not today. We make allowance on Sacred (Super) Bowl Sunday. That God must wait.

Well, next Sunday we will get back to normal. Other sporting events will soon take to their fields and the sacred festivals and their dance will go on. Some will be relieved that this 'god of the gridiron' will take leave for a spell, giving husbands and wives a chance to look at each other again. The family may even have time to take a ride in the country on a Sunday afternoon. Athletes with six and seven digits salaries will tend to surgery, business, and bank accounts. Those who pay the bills for such great worship will start their bidding wars for the best bodies. We devotees want it that way. That is the way we worship best. It is the blood-letting that draws us to the point of religious frenzy. We want a winner. We want a hero. We want a god! And it won't be a god worth a damn unless he wins; regardless of how many are helped off or carried off on a stretcher, there is always a fresh batch because of our need for a god—blood-soaked and sweat stained jerseys notwithstanding. It is all in the worship format—this carnage and blood.

Come to think of it, all really meaningful worship is determined by our understanding of the combination of 'carnage and blood.' In a couple of weeks the highly acclaimed and hotly controversial film, THE PASSION, starring Mel Gibson, will be released. I have been told it is full of the gruesome and the grotesque. A painful, up-close and personal look at the events during the last week of our Lord's life. It pulls no punches. You are there, so to speak! It will be difficult, I am told, to see the film as an innocent onlooker. Of course, the Cross of Christ has always been a hinge in history, a pivotal epoch in the sacred story. It is our salvation history! The film, Gibson surmised, could put an end to his acting career, but he said, "Something made me do it." He even bankrolled the making. He risked it all!

Long ago, on Calvary's hill, the line was drawn. You can choose the side you want to be on. The adversary has already staked his claim. We are not talking about a harmless scrimmage game. We are talking about 'life and death.' Heaven and hell battling it out! Don't get squeamish if 'carnage and blood' show up. And, in spite of all of that, final victory has already been predicted. So, let the whistle blow…and let's get on with the game! With PASSION!

February 24, 2004

He Left His Heart out on the Floor

"Thanks, Nick, for leaving your heart out there on the floor tonight." I have been struggling a couple of days about whether or not to write this because it is about my grandsons, Nick and Colton. Well, here I am in the middle of the night and can't sleep so please indulge me. Last Thursday evening the boys were playing a tournament game and wanted their 'Paps' to attend. It didn't look like we were going to be able to go and it disappointed my grandsons. But, on Thursday morning, by impulse more than anything else, Jane and I decided to drive the four hours over and catch the game and return early Friday morning. When we got to the gym right before the game, the boys were delightfully pleased to see us. We hugged. Nick said, "Good to see you Paps. I have a 'feel' about the game tonight. Even though this team has beaten us three times this year, I have a 'feel' about the game." And did he ever. It was a sight to behold, at least when seen through the lens of a grandfather. Nick made some unbelievable shots. They would have been the highlight film for ESPN. He played 'possessed.' He executed passes that were NCAA quality. He blocked out and rebounded shots from boys who were much larger and taller. He made eight assists that kept the score close. We all went a little nuts when we saw him come out from behind one of his teammates and lunge for a ball about to go out of bounds—airborne and almost horizontal with the floor, he managed to slap the ball back to a waiting player who drained it for three. I recall seeing a Larry Bird poster where he did about the same thing. The caption read: "I hate to see the ball go out of bounds." Larry Bird-like, Nick had a 'feel' for the game all right. And then it hit me.

I remember hanging a hoop in their backyard, when the boys could barely manage to shoot the ball three feet in the air. That makeshift arena became the launching pad for things to come. Even though it was just five feet above ground, we celebrated every shot as if we were engaged in the NCAA final. With their mini-sized basketball in hand, I would lift them up to the goal and they would throw the ball down through the hoop and then holler, "Swish, score." During the winter season, the Fisher-Price hoop stood in the living room, where the boys continued to perfect their shots. I could tell then, they had a 'feel' for the game.

Years later, when my grandsons lived across the street, we played basketball everyday. Lay-ups, foul shots, dribbling and shooting. Hour upon hour. While we went through this ritual day after day, I would tell the boys about the Indiana basketball mystique.

They would laugh at that because at that time they were Kentucky Wildcats and Rick Pitino was the greatest coach; Bobby Knight came in second. Little did I know what would come of all that time spent on McPheeters Drive playing street ball!

I still don't know, but for a moment or two last Thursday, something was unfolding before my eyes; and I was thanking God for the boys, for the game and for the 'hunch' that insisted we be on hand to see the spectacle. It was the kind of game where you have to cough or blow your nose to keep from crying, at least, for grandfathers. The game came 'down to the wire.' Nick and his Jr. Varsity team lost the game in points. Sometimes you don't get the most points, yet you still win. From across the gym I watched the team do the traditional slapping of hands, congratulating the winners and consoling the losers. I watched Nick. Head down. He walked briskly out of the 'cathedral' where he played as one who offered the sacrament of his best.

When we met a few minutes later, I saw something more sacred—he fell into his mother's arms and wept. A long, consoling embrace. It is moments like that about which books are written. I said some 'grandfather things' as we made our way to the car and the ride home. I thought it was going to be a long, silent ride home. When you feel things so deeply, the voice is the first thing to go. We were somewhat silent, and then Nick mustered up enough composure to tell us what the coach said. After the usual things a coach says after the last game of the season, he went from boy to boy with something to say so all could hear it. When he came to Nick, he whispered in his ear, "Nick, thanks for leaving your heart out there on the floor tonight." Through labored voice and heavy sobs, he got it out. What a gift! To be told you 'gave it your all, you played you heart out' is the kind of statement that will take a lifetime to unfold. I told Nick it just might be a long time before he ever hears something quite like that; and again, maybe not.

I told Nick again about the sign in the old gymnasium back home, there above the scoreboard it read: "When the Great Scorer comes to write against your name, he writes not about whether you won or lost but how you played the game."

I guess the message was intended to impress upon us young readers that basketball was something bigger than a game; that the game of basketball and the game of life are more than X's and O's. Grandson or no, a parable unfolded before us—Play the game with all your heart, give it your all! Thanks Nick, thanks for the memory! Thanks, too, for the 'feel' you had for the game and 'feeling' we all experienced in watching it get played-out…and we'll continue to watch it in a thousand different ways in the years to come. Swish, score!

March 10, 2004

The Passion

I have been putting off writing about THE PASSION. But, I have been listening– while it is grossing its millions, the whole country is talking about it. Just about anytime during the day you can get interviews, comments, critiques, and plaudits from every viewpoint via TV, newspaper, and the press. Anything from calling the film, 'obscene, pornographic, anti-semitic and an outrage' to elevating it to the status of biblical writ.

I was overwhelmed by the carnage and the cruelty. It was offensive to anyone's emotional equilibrium. If that is what Mel Gibson had in mind, he succeeded.

Well, Jesus was crucified! The Romans were good at it. And the Jews knew it! The sadistically cruel and utterly shameful death by crucifixion was used to uphold civil authority and preserve law and order against troublesome criminals, slaves, and rebels. In Palestine crucifixion was a public reminder of Jewish servitude to a foreign power. St. Paul did not exaggerate when he called the crucified Christ "a stumbling block to Jews and folly to Gentiles" (I Cor. 1:23). There is nothing in the Old Testament or in other Jewish sources to suggest that the Messiah could suffer such a fate. On the contrary, a crucified person—so far from being chosen, anointed, and sent by God—was understood to be cursed by God. To nonbelievers it seemed "sheer folly" to proclaim the crucified Jesus as God's Son, universal Lord, and coming Judge of the world. The extreme dishonor of his death by crucifixion counted against any such claims. Within a few years of Jesus' death it was considered utterly offensive for anyone to acknowledge the divine status of a crucified man.

Nothing expresses more forcefully the paradoxical Christian claims about the crucified Jesus than what Paul wrote about His death "even death on a cross" to indicate the extreme contrast between Christ's glory (Phil. 2:9-11), on the one hand, and the shameful death when he was crucified like a slave.

Well, here is my point—The notion of a "suffering Messiah" runs counter to what we know of messianic speculation in the first century; how much more an oxymoron a "crucified Messiah" must have seemed. Then…and now! I believe we have a Messianic problem. This film forces us to deal with Him again. *The Passion Of The Christ* is front and center! In two months, it will be halfway around the world. Don't be surprised if there are more attempts to crucify Him again! If Mel Gibson wanted to get us talking about it, it is happening. The question still remains for you and me: What are you going to do with Jesus?

Did you see Jeff Foxworthy the other night on Fox? In the midst of an hour-long 'back and forth' on the film, he finally said, "The thing we are not talking about tonight is the last thirty seconds of the film. The resurrection of the Christ authenticated every thing He said and did, even the crucifixion." There was stone silence. Maybe that is the next foray. The film mandates a sequel. I would encourage Mel Gibson to take some of his new wealth and do it. Of course, it probably would not have box-office appeal. Come to think of it, it was rather gory those first few hundred years and then we got civilized. Yeah, right!

March 16, 2004

The Thorn Birds

Do you remember the mini-series on TV, *The Thorn Birds*? If you were like me you didn't want to miss an episode. The Thorn Bird, so the legend goes, is a bird which sings only once in its life. It sings its single song more sweetly than any other creature on the face of the earth. From the moment it leaves its nest, the bird searches for a thorn tree and does not rest until it has found one. Having found its thorn tree the bird sings among the tree's savage branches and impales itself on the longest, sharpest spine. Then, dying, it rises above its own agony to out-carol the lark and the nightingale. The whole world stills to listen, and God in His heaven smiles. The best is bought at the cost of great pain, so says the legend.

This legend works itself out in the film series, *The Thorn Birds*. The priest (Richard Chamberlain) and Meggie (Rachel Ward) find their love for each other. Everyone in the film seems driven by circumstances beyond their control. Like the Thorn Bird, each person is driven to his or her fate. We catch something of such fatalism when we hear Meggie say, "We can know what we do wrong even before we do it, but self-knowledge can't affect or change the outcome."

Like the thorn birds, is everything in life foreordained around some compelling destiny over which we have no control? Are we driven, like the thorn birds, to impale ourselves on some thorn spine? Sin does play its havoc and there are times we wonder…but, no, we are not thorn birds, driven by blind fate—we can choose! We can say 'yes' or we can turn our backs on God and say, 'no'.

During this Lenten Season we are reminded that Jesus made choices…and by His obedience grants us succor and assistance. Tempted in every way as we are; yet without sin. Wow…the Eternal One, recognizing our frailty, our human predicament, announces that we are not thrown to the wind of chance and circumstance. He has entered into our pain and agony, becoming THE THORN BIRD (by choice), eventually impaling Himself on a cross, not by blind fate but with a free choice…and there sings the sweetest song we'll ever hear. And the whole world stills to listen and God in His heaven smiles! Meggie was right about one thing: "We can know what we do wrong even before we do it…" Where she needed some help was in recognizing that in spite of our wrong-doing, the 'outcome' can be changed by what Christ has done for us. I trust Lent had afforded us an opportunity to grasp

54

this incredible thought: GOD WAS IN CHRIST RECONCILING THE WORLD TO HIMSELF.

I hope we never get over it…that He had us in mind all along. Therefore, our Ultimate Thorn Bird, driven, not by blind fate, drank the cup of Calvary for the likes of you and me. And that, my friends, will make all the difference in the outcome.

March 22, 2004

The Church of Christ the Savior

At the end of our Lenten journey, we will be confronted with a cross! We have been hearing and reading much about the cross and the crucifixion these days…thanks to *The Passion Of The Christ*. The songwriter wrote about that '…emblem of suffering and shame…' St. Paul predicted and prophesized that it would be a 'stumbling block.' Sure enough, that is the case. As believers we confess that we belong to the 'church of Christ the Savior,' do we not? That means somewhere in the mix, there is a cross. And without that 'hinge of history' there is no Christianity. The Women's Division of the United Methodist Church is wondering whether or not we should use the cross as one of our symbols. After all, they say, the KKK uses the cross; the ancient crusades used crosses (and we know how wretched and evil they are to our memory). So what are we to do? Whatever case you want to make, for or against the symbol, there is a crucifixion. One cannot do an end run around it. The Cross…The Church of Christ the Savior, the both of them belong to the believer.

Several years ago, I was in Moscow. One of the incredible highlights of my tour of the city was the visit to the Cathedral of Christ the Savior. It was built over a century ago. Along came Stalin who despised the building and wanted it destroyed; the space was designated for the headquarters of the Communist Party. In the process of construction, they noticed that the building was sinking into the ground. So that plan was discarded and in its place was to be a large monument to Stalin. It was to be a massive structure of Stalin, so large that the belly section was to house a library. But, the ground began to sink. So all plans for any building were abandoned and a swimming pool was constructed that occupied the space. Stalin came and went.

When winds of reform came to Russia in the 90's, the land was given back to the church. The resources for the reconstruction came from people from all over Russia. That day, as I was watching the finishing of the Cathedral, an exact copy of the original, I asked my translator about the foundation. After all, the ground gave way in two previous building attempts. There was a long pause, and finally my translator said, "There is no explanation… It is the Church of Christ the Savior." That was it! It is true, you know. The Church of Christ the Savior cannot be destroyed. Attempts to eradicate its presence are futile. "On Christ the solid rock I stand, all other ground is sinking sand, all other ground is sinking sand." I used to sing that song. On that day, I *saw* that song. Can't really explain it…it is the Church of Christ the Savior! Jesus said that He would build His church and the gates of hell would not prevail. We just don't seem to get it. The 'gates of hell' have done their best and worst; after the smoke and fire, after the carnage scene has played its last act…I suppose, at its best, it is still 'sinking sand.' Every once in awhile, there will be attempts to 'blow the church to bits,' to erect some other more politically correct monument in its place, to replace the cross with a less offensive symbol—It is just not going to stay put! Can't explain it, except to say and to confess. IT IS THE CHURCH OF CHRIST THE SAVIOR! Cross, included!

April 5, 2004

Frost? at this Time of Year?

I was told at the Airport Restaurant this morning that there is a strong possibility of a killing frost tonight. You can get lots of tidbits at the Airport eatery. So Jane and I, wishing to protect our few blooms and buds, bedded them down in a warm blanket of mulch. After a long winter's sleep and a Spring that is being stubborn in its timing, the trees still stand barren and the things wanting to be green are banking their hopes on the warming of the sun. There ought to be a law of nature that prohibits such cruelty to itself.

In the Springtime of this Lenten Journey, with promises galore, this biting, blistering wind would do us in. And the Sun keeps shining, reminding us and the wind, "You can't take away the possibility. That belongs to me." And from that, we take courage. We will sink our roots deeper into the soil of our recovery and announce victory. And there will be fruit. Again and again and again. The wintry frost and the Sun will battle it out. That is what happens during Passion Week. And come Easter morning as we gather for a time for 'sunrise blessings,' there will be a certain 'chill in the air' and we will wonder why in the world we are up so early. When it is all over and we head towards our Easter sunrise breakfast, the Sun of Righteousness will burst forth. And we all of us will notice the 'warmth' and bid adieu to the chill that tried one last time to put a damper on the 'possibility.' And there will be fruit, again and again and again.

April 19, 2004

A Wise Woodcutter

The Easter Season has been a busy but blessed one! In many ways, we experienced a record-breaking day at the church. Maybe that is one reason why I have been silent. I still find it difficult to laud Easter's attendance. But, the Second Sunday of Easter has a way of bringing you back to reality. So what does a crowded church on Easter Sunday mean anyway? Like we are going for the gold, a record to put in the books? Have you ever heard about an unheralded record; something sizeable that, for the most part, has gone unnoticed? Let me tell you about one…right here in Mayodan, NC.

One of the first non-members I met after arriving here a couple of years ago was Harry Lemons. He is a man with a winsome witness. An unashamed carrier of the 'good news.' Always going about town, visiting the sick and shut-ins and making trips to hospitals and nursing homes to pray for them. I got the impression that the 'world was his parish', too. Unpretentious and gracious, he always graced his conversations with an affirming word. Then I heard about his father-in-law, F.C. Case.

Just a few old-timers remember Mr. Case; fewer still have any idea of the far-reaching impact this man had around the world. He was converted at the age of 16 and joined the church. Shortly after that, he attended a mission conference and felt the need to help distribute Christian literature around the world. He soon came in contact with Jack McAlister (via the radio) who had launched the World Literature Crusade. He was convinced that people could be brought to the Lord that way. Mr. Case's first contribution was $2.00. He wrote, "It is my ambition to provide the gospel for 10 million people before I die." He was told that $1000 could provide enough literature for one million people. How did he do it? He had no vehicle, only a mule and a wagon. He had no telephone and seldom ventured off his farm in the hills near Mayodan, NC.

He could feed his family of fifteen with pinto beans for $5 a month. He was frugal. He was sacrificial. During the depression he was sending WLC $10 a month. F.C. Case was a woodcutter. He spent his working life in the woods, cutting trees and chopping them into firewood. From the sales of his labor, he ended up as one of God's greatest 'paper missionaries'—sending literature; as he said, "I do it because it's going to win lost souls…" He reached his 'ten million people' before he died in 1976.

Jack McAlister once flew down from Canada to visit Mr. Case. He drove to Mayodan, looking for him. He had written but got no response. He even sent a telegram with the same result. The Director of the World Literature Crusade was determined to find the man who wanted to reach 10 million people before he died. He found him at an old farmhouse at the end of an old dirt road. McAlister recalled that the visit was one of the most rewarding experiences in his life. "I just cut wood…I love the woods…out there all by myself…I just love this work I am doing…God has been so good to me that I just can't turn Him down…"

I can picture this lonely, solitary figure walking through familiar forests, finding the right tree, laboriously felling and trimming it to usable sizes, then transporting it out of the woods on paths that existed only in his mind. Then I could envision that he was not alone at all. A crowd of ten million sat in a darkened stadium cheering him on with sounds that only he could hear.

He was a man who could hear eternal sounds. To him each movement of his saw meant someone would receive a gospel booklet and a chance to know Christ as his Savior.

McAlister wrote after his visit to Mr. Case's farm in Mayodan, "All God's heroes did not die in the first century. Remember F.C. Case in prayer; he's serving Christ in those hills near Mayodan, and thousands and thousands of people will be in heaven because of the dedication of this one man.

April 26, 2004

The Czar's Cannon

Last Sunday we celebrated Heritage Day at the church. On the official program calendar for the United Methodist Church, that is what we call it: Heritage Sunday. It is a time to reflect on our history, our past, present, and future. In the course of preparation for the day, I located some old pictures, interesting info, and some memorabilia that enhanced the celebration. I discovered several boxes of stained glass that once was a part of the Christ Window that graced the sanctuary before the tornado of 1998 destroyed the church. Members of the church were given those colorful pieces of glass as a reminder of our story. In developing the worship service, I discovered something else. This past Sunday, April 25, was the 50th Anniversary of my preaching/teaching ministry. When it came time to put the sermon together, I decided to preach about my favorite biblical character: Caleb. You guessed it, that 85 year old coot, who when asked what he wanted for an inheritance, pointed to the hills that were inhabited by the Anakims (giants) and said, "Give me that mountain!" While being careful not to equate myself to the likes of Caleb, I did call attention to the fact that God in His incredible amusing and amazing grace, led to this place, the mountains of Mayodan. Theologically, when one is doing what God wants you to do and you are doing it where He has lead, then that place is the greatest spot of the face of earth. And there is no place I'd rather be! I have been many places around the world. It has been a great run…but the lure of the Mayodan Mountain with whatever giants might be located in the environs, I will take. With what shall I arm myself for such battle?

Let me tell you a story—A few years ago I was in Moscow. On my tour of the Kremlin I came across a huge cannon, a monster of a gun, weighing 40 tons. The cannon balls each weighed, I was told, around a ton. It was cast iron, beautifully decorated with artwork that would grace a concert hall. There it stood and at its feet were a pile of cannon balls all ready and raring to go.

Then I was told it was called the Czar's Cannon, largely because of its size.

The cannon was never used. It has never fired because it was impossible to load it with sufficient powder to get the one-ton shots to leave the cannon chamber. "Why make such a cannon?" I asked. "Good question," I was told. "They would place this cannon at a strategic place so that when an invading army would approach they would see this formidable adversary and run for their lives. After all, a gun with these proportions would make a quick end of the enemy, so it was thought."

Well, I suppose it would work as a good strategy. I mean, size can be intimidating. To be outnumbered has never been an option for a ready military. Size has always made good, basic military sense. After all, victory often goes to the biggest and the mightiest.

"Have you seen the size of those giants?" That kind of a question can bring on forty years of wilderness wanderings. Mountains and giants are daunting, although every now and then a Caleb comes along and leads us in a seminar on how to conquer mountains. On occasion, a David shows up with a few small river stones and makes an astounding claim, not that Goliath is big, but that he is too big to miss! Ask Gideon and his three hundred and they'll testify that it isn't the size of the adversary that counts but the quality of your obedience. I mean, how do you feed a massive crowd of 5000 with a sack lunch? It is ludicrous, the kind of problem that would make anyone run. Ask those Israelites marching around the Jericho walls with no artillery at all, except trumpets and water pitchers. "What is your plan? How are you going to get past those massive walls?" we asked. I can hear them saying, "Watch us make thirteen trips around the walls…the rest belongs to he One who gave the orders."

It has always been like that, I suppose. It doesn't matter how hot the fiery furnace and how many lions assemble in your corner, the Czar's Cannon does not have the last word. In fact, it has no word at all! I don't know why I keep living as though it did. I see the foe and fear comes creeping in, telling me to run. When will I ever get it? To realize that there is not enough powder in hell to make any kind of a charge against the fragile faith that still believes that bread can be broken and blessed; that in the midst of the fire there is a Fourth; and that giants drop to their knees in defeat before the claim that one comes "in the name of the Lord."

The Czar's Cannon cannot destroy me, but running from it will! The devil's plan is to get us bogged down in the fruitless and futile task of sizing him up. Once we do that he can almost chalk up a victory. So what are we to do? Make thirteen trips around the enemy if you have to, but take your feeble, wobbling legs and walk on past the cannon. Take your small lunch and a few river stones…and announce for God's sake that the Czar's Cannon is the one defeated and it might as well be "beaten into plowshares and pruning hooks."

I like Caleb. Optimistic. Up for it! "Give me that mountain." Giants, notwithstanding! Fifty years of this and I still have life to go…in the Mayodan mountains.

May 3, 2004

The Sacrament of Holy Communion…Revisited

The first Sunday of the month we celebrate Holy Communion at Mayodan United Methodist Church. Last Sunday's worship service with Holy Eucharist was felt deeply by many. On his way out of church Sunday, Billy Sechrist said to me, "Of all the Sunday's, the times we have Holy Communion are the most meaningful to me." I don't think I have ever heard that kind of comment before. It caught me somewhat off guard, but I honestly replied, "Me, too."

I've been thinking about that for the last couple of days. Holy Eucharist.

My mind went back to a communion service I had in Estonia. My inadequate hands broke the bread along with the other clergy in attendance and then individually we walked among the congregants and passed out the bread. Then, I held the cup and passed it as each drank from the common cup, saying, "The blood of Christ for you." I said it over and over again. Maybe to 100 people. Looking into the eyes of each recipient, announcing 'the blood of Christ for you' does something inside you.

After all were served, the custom at the end of Eucharist was to join hands, the whole congregation being connected, bodily. I made my way down front, right near the communion table. There was an old man there, watching and listening to me intently. I took his hand and with both of his he grasped mine. He was not drunk be he did have the smell of alcohol on him. I noticed the grimaces of some of the saints sitting on the front row, that this man was getting front-of-the-church billing. It is hard sometimes to embrace the unseemly. I tried it and put my arm around his shoulder. He snuggled in closer, looking up to me with a radiant smile, kind of like the smile that comes over you when you realize something lost got found. When the service was over he wanted to show me something. He pulled up his trouser on his left revealing an ugly wound, wrapped in blood-soaked rags, and wondered if I could assist him with some medicines. He asked for a dollar. You can't do much with a dollar, I thought. I gave him $10, and then I smelled the alcohol again. My suspicions were aroused. 'There goes my $10 bucks.' I told him no alcohol…find some food and medicines. I suppose that made me feel better. He assured me that would be the case. Who knows?

This business of befriending 'winebibbers' is tough stuff. And you would think that in light of such a beautiful morning and a moving sacramental service, you shouldn't have to deal with the unkempt and those reeking with alcohol. But there he was; the one closest to the Eucharist Table. That is the way it is sometimes—the one closest to the Table is often the most needy.

Sometimes your neat little categories and well-ordered litanies come unraveled and you stand in the presence of need. I don't know what became of him…where my ten dollars went…whether he abused the trust…what the 'bread and wine' meant to him; but of this I am certain, that Jesus died for him, that there is redemption in the Meal, that grace can sober him into reality and that one day…he will remember and be thankful. The one closest to the Table is often the most needy! I know that for a fact, for as I broke that bread and passed the cup, I was praying, "Lord, cleanse me. Forgive me. Make me. Use me." The Eucharist was for me on that morning long ago. Outcasts and winebibbers, the whole wild lot of us—all eating and drinking from the same Table. That is the way it is. That is the way it was back there on that cold Sunday morning…that is the way it was this past Sunday. Every once in awhile the pastor will get some confirmation that of all Sundays, Holy Communion Sunday is the most meaningful. It is more than the liturgy. It is the pulling up of chairs to His Table, having the audacity to 'eat and drink' and remember. And when that happens, you experience something that transcends the moment. It is that 'transcending' that gives power and meaning to the embracing of the unkempt and those reeking with the smell of alcohol…to the offering of $10 in Jesus' name for food and medicine. Because I, too often disheveled in spirit and possessing the fragrance of an ill-mannered demeanor, find myself closest to the Table, the neediest of all, 'drinking and eating' for healing and wholeness. Of all Sundays, Holy Communion is the most meaningful. Thanks Billy!

May 11, 2004

Priceless Moments

This past week I had a few 'priceless moments'—like kneeling down by Lucy Lee Martin's wheelchair and saying the Lord's Prayer together; like praying with Ruth Barksdale and after finishing she remarked, "I like the way you finished that prayer." I finished it by saying, "…now Lord, we are confident that Ruth Barksdale is safe in the arms of Jesus." And she repeated it, "Ruth Barksdale, safe in the arms of Jesus." You can't purchase moments like that! Have you done the kind of reflecting lately that brought to mind a 'priceless moment?' Let me tell you a story that occurred to me a few years ago…

Patrick loved his red hat. Everywhere Patrick went the hat was sure to go. He ate with it on, worshipped, even went to sleep with his hat firmly anchored over his golden hair. The hat's bill usually concealed green eyes that, if you could see them would melt your heart. I rarely saw Patrick without his hat. While I loved the boy, it was his worn and faded hat that often attracted my attention and the hat gave me first entry into that young imaginative life. "Patrick, I sure do love that hat. I'd give a dollar for a hat like that. Would you take a dollar for that hat, Patrick?" And he would answer quicker than I could ask the question, "No way!" Of course, no way. Something that important isn't for sale. Over time I upped the bid. Still no sale. One day I held out a twenty dollar bill. I would have done it. It took him a second longer this time, but Patrick's answer was firm. "No way!" "Well, how much will it take?" I asked. And he said, "Maybe a million bucks."

Well, at the seminary senior banquet, when his mother was graduating, she gave a brief speech. Finally, she asked that Patrick come forward and stand on a chair beside her. She thanked him, her six-year-old Patrick, for his support and love. Then she did the strangest thing. She called out my name and invited me to come forward. I was nervous. What was she going to do? Why me? There in front of 350 people, with young Patrick standing on the chair beside her, she said, "Dr. Killian, for the past three years, every time you saw Patrick with his hat on, you would say…?" And I said it, "I'll give you a dollar for that hat, Patrick." She then turned to Patrick and said, "And what did you say, Patrick?" And Patrick bellowed out, "No way!" He grinned from ear to ear. She let silence settle in for an awkward pause before she spoke again. "Patrick wants to give you something, Dr. Killian." Somehow I knew that I was about to receive the little red hat. All kinds of emotions tumbled through my mind and heart. A thousand heartbeats said, "No, he mustn't." But he did. With another pause, he grinned up at me. I will never forget that green-eyed look. "Chuck, I want you to have this hat. You will take good care of it, won't you?"

For one who struggles over receiving a gift, overwhelmed and taken aback by such a gesture, I whispered to Patrick, "I'll give it back after the program." He shook his head. His 'no' meant this was for keeps. I knew what that hat meant to him, and I would soon find out what it meant to me. A million dollar hat—free! A gift, and I thought of giving it back? When will I learn? It's for you, Chuck. Free. Don't try to figure it out. Quit thinking of others more deserving of this hat. He gave it to you. I hugged the giver. It was all that I could do. I promised him, "I'll take care of it, Patrick." I knew that as the years would roll by, the story of Patrick's little red hat would generate more power than the gift itself.

Folks, there are times when I confess that I don't deserve such gifts. And the Spirit keeps reminding me that it is for me. "I don't want you to deserve it, I just want you to receive it." I'll never understand such giving, but gifts are like that. Even a little red hat. Even hearing the sound of Lucy Lee's crackled voice as she utters the Lord's Prayer, and hearing the sound of Ruth Barksdale's affirmation that she was 'safe in the arms of Jesus' was nothing short of being 'priceless.' Priceless moments are all around us…are you listening?

May 24, 2004

A Moses Moment

Last Friday evening, Jane and I returned to Wilmore, KY, to attend my retirement dinner from Asbury Seminary. After 34 years of teaching, I got a dinner and a lovely retirement chair—plus much more. My daughter, Elaine, was there to speak on behalf of the family. What a stirring, yet undeserved tribute she paid her father. It was indeed a hallowed moment. Reg Johnson, my colleague and soul-friend, gave a tribute as well. The following is what I said…

I used to sit under the old walnut tree back home and dream of faraway places." Grandpa would ask, "Got any dreams?" "Yeah, I'm dreaming about Pittsburgh." Grandpa wanted to know about that dream. "Well," I said, "Cy Sarber drives his semi to Pittsburgh three times a week and I want to see the world…I want to see Pittsburgh." "Well," grandpa would say, "on the other side of Pittsburgh."

I have been thinking about that lately—life on the other side of Pittsburgh. When one comes to a critical crossroad, a transition point, you tend to think back and look ahead. It was like I was having a 'Moses Moment.' Moses had been wandering forty years in the wilderness. He really got a little 'long in the tooth' and God tells him it is time to say goodbye. Can't you imagine Moses, standing with a pained expression, saying, "God, just exactly what did you have in mind, when we spoke so long ago?" That has been my Moses-feeling in recent days. I have thought back through my forty years of wanderings around in the ministry. Sometimes barely surviving, hanging on by my fingertips, listening to the murmuring students and parishioners, and then being told it is getting time to say 'goodbye' to this chapter of ministry.

Goodbye transitions were not easy for Moses. Me, either! Letting go, losing grip, preparing to exit…it is hard word. I think you have to prepare and cultivate your eye for miracles as well as have an ear for the future. You have to learn to say goodbye to some things in order to say hello to others. You have to look for God in the exits.

He was wandering around with them for forty years. Sometimes bad, sometimes good. I suppose there were times when he could have said, "This isn't what mother had in mind when she left me to be brought up by Pharoah's daughter. I could have made it in Egypt. I am a pretty good outward-bound kind of a person; good, too at politics."

Rabbi Kushner reminds us that God has assigned to each of us a certain role, and it's the only one you are going to get. "Sometimes we don't like our parts, wish we were someone else." I had visions of theatre. (Someone said I ought to go to Hollywood. When I told Grandpa that, he said that I should go, too…the walk would do me some good.) Wanted to be a baseball player. But God said, "Those parts are already taken by Robert Redford and Cal Ripken. You are going to be a preacher. You want it or not?"

When exits and entrances appear in our lives, we often miss the small miracles that come with those times. We usually want to hold on tightly to the familiar; we want more. We fail to realize the truth that when one door closes another opens. And God is at both, in the beginnings and endings. When we say 'yes' to God, the miracles comes. Little did I know tha content of the 'miracle'—the miracle of being placed in Mayodan. The past two years have been a good season in our lives. Jane and I could not have been more wonderfully placed. The miracle is not so much in what is occurring in Mayodan but what is happening in us.

This has been a God-appointed thing God has done. And we are journeying into the 'miracle of His grace'.

E.E. Cummings summed up life. "...with you I leave the remembrance of miracles." I leave with you the remembrance that we have touched over the years; sometimes the touch was light and subtle; sometimes over a chasm of pain and agony...but we have touched. I am content to let others say what little there is to be said about how I might have touched others. I leave you with the remembrance of small miracles. I leave you with the sadness and the extreme gratitude for those moments together when we glimpsed the Promise Land. And I leave you with the knowledge that God is not finished with us yet. So, let me offer my prayer one more time. "Lord, just exactly what was it you had in mind when we talked so long ago? Would you please go over that, just one more LIFE. Slowly. Amen."

It has been a great trip to Pittsburgh and beyond! It is the 'beyond' that thrills me most...and at the present time, it is spelled: MAYODAN.

July 7, 2004

A Gift Most Precious

Someone asked me the other day, over a cup of coffee, "Chuck, why do you do what you do? How in the world did you end up in Mayodan?" I never gave it much thought until, this week, I was asked again, "How in the world did you end up in Mayodan?" I am not quite sure what is meant by that question. Could they be saying, "Why would you want to come to Mayodan?" or "Why would a bishop send you to this place?" or "How did you find your way to Mayodan?" or "Of all the places in the world you could go, why Mayodan?" or simply, "Isn't it amazing how God works...and here you are in Mayodan?" There are more times than I would like to admit that I wondered about God's calling me into the ministry. There are probably many good reasons why God shouldn't have called me in the first place. But I am in good company. Moses stuttered. David's armor didn't fit. Jonah ran from God. Samson had long hair. Abraham was too old. Lazarus was dead. Naomi was a widow. Gideon doubted. On and on...But God didn't require a job interview. He just took me as I was and said He would make mincemeat of my limitations. And as for being in Mayodan, I didn't have much to do with that. I settled that issue a long time ago. "Where He leads me, I will follow." All of this made me remember a story....

> One of the ancient kings of Persia loved to mingle with his people in disguise. Once, dressed as a poor man, he descended the long flight of stairs, dark and damp, to the tiny cellar where the fireman, seated on ashes, was tending the furnace. The king sat down beside him and began to talk. At meal time the fireman produced some coarse black bread and a jug of water and they ate and drank. The king went away but returned again and again for his heart was filled with sympathy for the lonely man. They became very good friends as time passed. At last the king thought, "I'll tell him who I am, and see what gift he will ask.' So he did, but the fireman didn't ask for a thing. The king was astonished and said, 'Don't you realize that I can give you anything—a city, a throne?' The man gently replied, 'I understand, you Majesty. You could give nothing more precious. You have given yourself and that is far more than I could ever deserve."

A glass of cold water given in His name makes a shambles of kingly robes and gilded mansions. So, I respond to those questions: Why not Mayodan? Since God is in it, obedience has a way of freeing one from the temptation to offer, as did the king in this story, that which was barely more than a mess of pottage. The best that I can ever come up with in this ministry stuff is to sit and munch on coarse bread and drink musty water. And here and there, now and then, someone finds the way…and I end up receiving far more that I could ever deserve. As an old sage put it, "If you love what you do, you'll never work a day in your life."

July 9, 2004

Sold to God

I shall not soon forget the incredible memorial and celebration service this past Monday, when over 175 people gathered at the Mayodan United Methodist Church to give thanksgiving to God for the life and witness of Ruth Tesh Barksdale. For two hours prior to the start of the service people gathered to pay their respects in the manner that Ruth would have loved. There were tears. Stories. Pictures. Laughter—lots of laughter. We all remembered Ruth's cleansing laughter. Ruth cut a wide swath in the community. People from all walks of life were there; churched and unchurched, city and county officials, friends from far and near, Baptists, Moravians, Presbyterians (Ruth possessed a large 'faith family'), and a myriad of folks (who stood in for thousands, I suppose), who were touched by this one solitary life.

I mentioned that it was my privilege and joy to be her pastor, although I came into her life at the 'finishing line'. Resolutely, she hung onto life as a treasured possession and would not let it go! One does not live the way Ruth lived and let it all go with a turn of the head; no, Ruth took her days in a stride that suggested each day was a gift and she would receive it as such. A gift! She was one of God's great gift-givers. Even in her last 'silent days' she 'spoke' to me. After one of my visits to Ruth, when I sat in that 'sacred silence' of waiting, it came to me that Ruth had something to say. Oh, she couldn't speak, but she did. Inaudible, to be sure, but in my imagination I heard her. It went something like this…

"Chuck, the house that I have been living in is 89 years old. It has lost some of its original color, and much of the red and pink are gone. It doesn't stand quite as straight as it once did. Why, this old house has looked up and down a thousand corn rows; and hoed a many. This old house housed and cradled four wonderful children, and embraced them with the joy of living. This old house has rumbled with delight and has been shaken with laughter. It has known the sweetness of tender love and has been torn with storms and turbulence. Sometimes, the old house seemed like it could be shattered by pain and difficulty, but has stood the test. This old house has been with friends aplenty…has known agony…been repaired by specialists. It has stored away secrets, revered and treasured. The attic is full of memories. Why, someday, Pastor Chuck, they will be taken out and remembered. There are many rooms in this house. One very special room is the heart-room, where all my loves are stored, where the compassion, the hurts, the triumphs, and the exquisite passions for those I love are stored. I have a sacred room, too. Hanging there on the walls of my soul, I suppose, are the pictures, mementoes, plaques, even the voices of thousands who visited that room. I look at the house and I see an aging house needing a coat of paint, but covered with the bushes and trees of experience, willing to stand sturdy until the end. Pastor Chuck, 89 years ago my parents gave me deed to this house with the understanding that I use it and enrich it. I have done so, and it deserves my thanks. It is a house now crammed with many memories, but still it stands staunch and valiant waiting until it must finally close with a sign saying SOLD TO GOD."

August 12, 2004

With a Name Like That...

I regret that is has been far too long since I last made an entry with my "Ramblings." I must get caught up with this discipline or it will escape me. This summer has been far too busy, taking me around the country: preaching, teaching, partying and playing with my grandchildren.

In June, Jane and I were in Ludington, MI where I was the preacher for Epworth Assembly. It was a wonderful gathering of Methodists from all over the country who 'summer' on the lake. It was an incredibly beautiful place. One afternoon, we decided to go to Pentwater, a small village that caters to tourists with their craft shops and eateries. Somewhat tired, I found a bench on which to sit, awaiting Jane's return from shopping. I saw a young man pushing a baby buggy coming down the street. I noticed he spied an empty space beside me and I invited him to sit down. I remarked that the baby appeared to be far more contented then he was; that he needed some rest. He thanked me and sat down. We engaged in the usual stuff—the baby's name was Christina and his wife was Ella. "Where are you from?" I asked. "Orrville, Ohio," he responded. I informed him, as if he didn't know, that that was the birthplace of Bobby Knight. Being a Hoosier, we all know gobs of basketball trivia. He was quick to answer, "Yes, Bobby Knight! My aunt was his English teacher and she didn't like him." We changed the subject. He said, "You know, Bobby Knight is not Orrville's only claim to fame." I wondered what else could come out of Orrville. "It is the home office for Smucker's." I was quick with a quip, "With a name like that it has got to be good." I tried to sound original. We laughed. He said he worked for Smucker's and was there doing quality control.

On our trip to Pentwater we passed acres and acres of cherry orchards. "Yes," he said, "I am here to check on the cherry crop.

I will take my report back to corporate headquarters next week." It sounded a tad silly, but wanting to discover more substance to our conversation, I asked, "Does Smuckers have a mission statement (we Methodists are into mission statements)?" "In fact, we do" he said. He mentioned five aspects of Smucker's mission: Ethics, Quality, Independence, Growth and People. I told him that that explained why he was there, concerned about the 'quality' aspect of their mission. He smiled and said, "That is so." I noticed he was wearing a company shirt, 'Smucker's' embroidered on his left sleeve. For some strange reason I asked him his name: "Reid Smucker. My uncle is president of the company." I now become even more interested in checking out the substance of where our conversation was headed. I got him to tell me something of the Smucker story.

"In the early 19th Century, John Chapman "Johnny Appleseed' wandered the Ohio countryside, sowing apple seeds and securing a place in American legend. It was from the fruit of Johnny Appleseed's trees that my great grandfather, Jerome Monroe Smucker pressed cider at the mill he opened in 1897. Later, he prepared apple butter, which he sold from the back of a horse-drawn wagon.." They have come a long way.

Here I sat alongside an heir to the fortune and he is there in Pentwater checking out the quality of the cherries and will report back next week. Before we left, he asked me what my favorite fruit was. Blueberries. "I brought with me two jars of blueberry jelly. One is for the manager of the farm where we will visit tomorrow. Would you like the other?" He went to his van, brought a jar of blueberry jelly and gave it to me. And like a kid wanting a big league signature, I wondered if he minded signing my jar of Smucker's blueberry jelly. He was gracious. It sits in the fridge now, waiting for the day when I will 'taste and see' something of 'quality control.'

Now, a month away from that experience I am still pondering that mission statement—ethics, quality, independence, growth, and people. It could serve as a mission statement for the church, too! It could be said, couldn't it, that the church is to be characterized by: Character, Our Best, Singularly Focused, Reaching out, and Caring. If the corporate mindset is so determined, should not the Church of Jesus Christ be likewise <u>driven by faithful</u>ness to get our Product out across the country and around the world? We have been called and claimed by a magnificent obsession through Jesus Christ—with a Name like that, it has got to be good!

August 18, 2004

Hummingbirds and Homing Pigeons

My wife, Jane, loves to bird-watch. It is called ornithology. Which reminds me that I took that class back in college under Dr. Hobson, who had us get up at five in the morning and go out in the woods and watch the birds wake up. We were to journal about our findings. Sometimes she would go with us, and I still can't get over how she would 'ooooh' and 'aaaahh' at every sound, even though the birds were unseen. It was like a spiritual experience for her. Well, I never did cotton to watching for birds in the dark, so I dropped the class and found another course that met at a decent hour that didn't require binoculars and tape recorders. To this day, a bird is a bird is a bird. Not for Jane. She has books all around the house; books that identify what she is observing on the porch or out the window. "Oh, did you see that bluebird?" One that she couldn't recognize was soon identified by her handy-dandy *Pictorial Guidebook to the Birds of the World.* She would spot the early spring arrivals and bid goodbye to the last ones to leave in the fall. And her feeding the Mayodan winter dwellers usually filled the front and back yards.

The other day I was sitting on my deck and all of a sudden I heard a murmuring, humming sound. Just a few feet away, hanging from the gutter, was a hummingbird feeder. Red of course, with red sugar water in it. And there was this little bird, feeding. No sooner had it come, than it left. Then, back again. A few minutes later, the same. Then I remembered Dr. Hobson's opening lecture. "Birds are God's fanciful art work," she would say or something to that effect. Art work, indeed. So I decided to find out more about hummingbirds and something of god's 'art work.' I discovered that they can fly to the right, to the left, up and down. They have legs too small to use except for perching. If they want to travel two inches, they have to fly. They flap their wings about fifty times a second, fly anywhere from 30-60 mph. Many migrate annually over 2000 miles. They feed every ten minutes and can consume 2/3 their body weight daily. They weigh about 3 grams and live to be about 12 years old. They are 3 inches in length but big enough to take on a blue jay. Did you know that there are over 50 species of flowers that would never get pollinated if it were not for the hummingbird? Well, there you have it—a hummingbird in the ecological system, doing its part. Indeed, a 'work of art.' Thank God for hummingbirds.

The other day I was visiting with my friends, Dot and Ralph Joyce. Ralph was in the back in one of his sheds. In the course of our conversation I learned that Ralph used to raise homing pigeons. For someone who never liked ornithology, I knew little about homing pigeons; wasn't even sure how to spell it. So I asked Ralph about the spelling. "Just like it sounds, Home. Homing." Duh, Chuck. I wondered why they called them that. "Well, you train them in their familiar environment, they get used to their home. There is something in their bloodstream, I suppose. You never have to cage them. They know where they live and they are comfortable where they live and never forget their home." Ralph offered that with the assurance that the discussion was over. But, no, I had more questions. "What if you took them fifty miles away and let them loose?" Ralph smiled and said, "I have done that many times. Once, I did that and they beat me home." "How?" I inquired. "There is something in the magnetic field that gets locked in their memory and unless there is some outside interference, they'll make their way home." He told me about one man who took a bird to Florida and three days later it was home. Well, there you have it, again. Some of God's 'fanciful art work'.

I liked what Ralph said about the homing pigeon 'having something in the bloodstream' that causes the bird to head home. God made us for two worlds. There is instilled deep within us all a hunger, a thirst, a 'God-like reason' that longs for home. We used to sing it: "This world is not my home, I'm just a passing through..." We all possess an inner-field of energy, God-like thirsting for what is to come. Life is kind of like the training of a homing pigeon. You create in them a thorough liking for their environment, their home, their surroundings; and when it comes time for the test—there is no fooling them. Home, they head! Is life little more than probation, getting comfortable with life, living and the pursuit of holiness? And when the final BIG TEST comes—we all will know our way home. Because deep within us God has placed a restlessness until we finally rest in HIM.

God has gobs of art work all around us. Take note of it, even the birds. "Life is for the birds!"

September 29, 2004

September 28 and 391 Years

Lucille Reid was 102 years old yesterday, September 28th. In June, Odessa Holt turned 102. Eva Richardson is 95 and Gertrude James, 92. I visited them yesterday...it took most of the day. Total years of life experience: 391. Like a newspaper reporter I went in quest for a 'story'.

First stop: Lucille Reid. I had visited with her in the past and was looking forward to our time together again, on this her birthday. You don't get to talk to centenarians very often, especially those whose mind is still alert, sharp, and inquisitive. Lucille is in charge of current events at Eden Estates. Her group gets together once a week to talk about what is going on in the world. She was a teacher for nearly 40 years and those who sat under her teaching have never forgotten it. So I asked her, "What was your philosophy of teaching?" She said it was to give the students a good foundation and 'fill in the blanks' that they did not get at home. When I asked a former student of hers what it was like to be in her classroom, all he said was, "We had to memorize the 100th Psalm. You know the one about 'make a joyful noise unto the Lord...serve the Lord with gladness...enter into his gates with thanksgiving...the Lord is good and his truth endureth for all generations'." For that one student, it stuck!

"And what has been your philosophy of life, Lucille?" She quickly responded, "Simple living and good parents" She talked about her Methodist roots "...although I am an Episcopalian, I am a Methodist at heart. I made my profession of faith at a little church in Millbrook, near Raleigh. I don't think that little church is still around, but what happened to me there, is!" What an incredible faith statement. Her final words to me were: "I have had a happy life. No serious health problems. And they tell me, the best is still coming." We prayed together. The best is still coming!

Second stop: Odessa Holt. Quite feeble, yet alert, Odessa was so appreciative of my visit. Though her voice was weak, her mind was strong and her words were penetratingly focused. I asked her the same questions. To what do you attribute your long life? "The good Lord who is merciful...and how you treat other people." Then, I got her to recall some of her fondest memories. "You may not think this very important, Pastor, but when I was a little girl, growing up on the farm—we were poor. One summer there was a drought; our crops were shriveling up. There was no rain. Grandma came over to our house and told us children some stories in hopes of lessening our fear and uneasiness. One evening when I was driving the cows to the barn from the field, I came across a stump and I was impressed to pray for rain. I knelt there and prayed for rain. Within 24 hours we had a most wonderful rain. It was like liquid pieces of crystal falling from heaven. Standing on the porch, watching the rain, I realized two things: We will have something to eat, and God answers prayers." "How did you come to faith?" I inquired. "When I was 12, I remember walking to church in Providence, Virginia. They were having a revival. I heard the gospel, simple and appealing. When the minister said if anyone wanted to receive Christ, they should come forward, I did. I joined the church that night. Grew up in the church. Came to Mayodan in 1929, where I taught Sunday School at the Methodist Church. But you know something, I am looking forward to the time when the Lord calls me to be with Him, and until then I want to do what he wants me to do. Then I can go 'home'." Her favorite song is "I love to tell the story" and we sang a verse of that as best we could. I finished my visit by asking, "What would you tell the young who might inquire for some advice?" She said, "Do what you can do, but always look before you leap." We prayed together. I left with the feeling that Odessa did a lot of looking before leaping…and always did what she could.

Third stop: Eva Richardson. I visit Eva at Brittaven about once a month. Eva is one of the great saints in the church. She and her sister, Annie, were faithful and reliable witnesses for Christ and staunch supporters of the Mayodan United Methodist Church. They got it honestly from their parents. No one in the history of this church is more highly revered than Mr. and Mrs. Luther Richardson. But Eva, in many ways, is gone. Alzheimer's has played a cruel trick on this saint. She spends her days in her wheel chair, ambling slowly around the corridors that imprison her. Most of the time, she sits in her room, starring at three pictures on her nightstand—one of her and Annie, one of her parents, and one of Eva and me. That picture was taken when Eva was able to come to the church over a year ago. She was so happy that day. She told the congregation that it was the 'best day of her life'. Six times in that short visit on the 28th, she asked me if I had seen those pictures. Six times, I pointed them out again to her: you and your sister, your parents, and you and your pastor. "Everybody has been real good to me," were her last words before we had prayer. I prayed and then she prayed for me. "Dear God, bless the church, the pastor and all the wonderful people…" There was a long pause. I was waiting for her to continue. I looked down at her and she looked up at me, pointing to the three pictures. "Have you seen those pictures? That is my father, Luther, and my mother, Lou (I think that is her name)." I gave one last look at the three pictures and told her that I loved her and would be back soon. She smiled…and returned to her world of pictures—her life, her family and her church.

Fourth stop: Gertrude James. I had been promising Gertrude that we would go and get some ice cream. Last Sunday, we made a date for the 28th, late afternoon. Per usual, Gertrude, at 92, was out sweeping the sidewalk. She was waiting for her preacher to get there. She remembered we had a date. "I'll lock the door, you finish sweeping, and off we'll go," she said. And we did. My left elbow served as her walking cane. We got into my pickup and off we went to the Airport Restaurant for a dish of ice cream. We didn't talk about too much, just enjoyed being together and enjoying each other's presence over a small dish of vanilla ice cream. She told me that what has kept her going was <u>hard work and reasonably good health</u>. And when I asked her about becoming a Christian, she replied (as if it just happened yesterday), "When I was eleven (that was 80 years ago) I attended a Baptist revival and was 'urged and begged' to go the altar. I did and it looks like what got started years ago is still working." (She smiled and cackled one of her patented laughs). For Gertrude, something is still working. When the Tuesday date was over, I walked her to her door, put the rest of her uneaten ice cream in the freezer, said a prayer and left. "Bless your heart," she said. That has always been <u>Gertrude's</u> benediction. <u>Bless your heart</u>.

So what of the 391 years of life experiences? What did I learn about life? What did these four incredible women have to say to me in summary?

Lucille—Live the simple life and be good parents.
Odessa—God answers prayers.
Eva—In the final analysis all we have is our earthly family and our family of faith.
Gertrude—Bless those around you.

Following this recipe, you might not live to be 102—you just might live forever

October 4, 2004

I Am Still Praying for Patience

I am delighted when I hear someone say, "The Lord has delivered me and given me victory over...(a number of things)." I wonder why, after about fifty years, I am still waiting to be 'delivered' and be given 'victory' over my impatience. Being patient has not been one of my sterling virtues. I suppose I get it honestly. My father always seemed to be running while he was working. He was a painter. With a gallon in hand, he would actually scamper up the ladder to get at it. I can still hear him saying to me, "move, move, move". In other words, get on with it; often bellowing, "If it is worth doing—do it well and do it right NOW!" He was always sweating, even in the winter. He'd tell me of the days of the depression: how it affected him; how one would have to hustle to make ends meet; how it made you look around and observe. And he did that right well. He could spot potential dollars away off…old worn out tractors in a field, nearly buried in weeds and honeysuckle. We would stop and before long, we would be pulling the junker home to be 'scrapped out' for a few dollars. If he thought a barn needed painting, he'd stop and offer the farmer a deal and I would end up mixing paint (back in the days of linseed oil and turpentine). He would carry a magnet in his pocket, because he said you never know when you have to decide between brass and copper. "Haste makes waste?" No, dad would say "If you don't hurry up, you'll get wasted." Dad had perfected the art of filling an hour with 120 minutes worth of energy. Even when we traveled to relatives, he'd brag on the fact that we beat the last trip's time—"Well, we made it in two hours and 23 minutes, knocking off three minutes from the old record." He'd sharpen the hoe so sharp that it could cut off your toe (and often my toes were bloody). "It makes the job go faster." Once he heard a sermon and remarked, "If he'd left out all the non-essentials, we could have been home and had dinner by the time he finished." Personal worth was tied to your capacity for not permitting "the grass to grow under your feet." Well, such is my heritage!

Today, I went to K-Mart to buy a sheet of poster board. That was it. Found it and went to the check out. This will be quick, I thought. Yeah, right! Fifteen checkout counters and one light on. In that line there were about ten people waiting. I saw several of those red-aproned employees having their coffee break, oblivious to my plight. I thought I would try the one-hour photo desk and was told it was closed for film processing and if I could read the sign I wouldn't have needed to ask; at least that was what that look from the clerk inferred. I left my place in line and scouted for one of those 'ten-items or less' lines. There was none. By the time I got back to the one operational checkout, I was now farther back in line, much to the glee of those who watched the plotting of my strategy to find a quick exit.

You look longingly at the clerk, craning your neck, wondering why it is taking so long. Then you discover someone wants a price check (the bar code is missing). The clerk leaves us all stranded there as she goes the length of the front of the store looking for the telephone. We hear the message, "need a price check on a Tonka truck", then someone wants to pay with a personal check. The store wants three pieces of personal identification and the person only has two. The store manager is summoned. While he is there I have the nerve to inquire, "Why the holdup?" Only one checkout clerk, why? The manager was kind and gentle. He said, "Syd did not come in today. I don't know why. We are short-handed." I said, "Give me Syd's telephone number and I will call and find out." Half in jest and half in frustration, the manager found it mildly humorous. Finally, another light went on and three customers hurried over to that line ahead of me. Would you believe it—one of the customers wanted to fill out a credit application or some contest questionnaire. When I finally got to the clerk with my one piece of poster board, she asked, "What is you zip code?" "What is my zip code?" You want to know my zip code before I purchase this $.79 piece of poster board?" "Yes." Why?" "I don't know" "I don't think I am going to give you my zip code." (Pause) "You don't know why you want my zip code?" "I think it is some survey they are doing." I said, "It is a good thing that K-Mart is doing a survey; I can understand it, because if this kind of service continues most of your customers are going to be out-of-state."

With my poster board in hand, I headed to the jewelry department to get a band for my watch. I found one. $5.95. "I will take that one. Please, would you put the band on my watch?" And the clerk said, "Sorry, we can't do that." "You can't do that. The last band I bought here, they put it on for me." "Can't do that anymore. Company policy." "Then keep it. I don't want it." She probably had customers like that before, and I read that look from her that seemed to say, "I work here for minimum wage and I don't care if you buy it or not." I thought to myself, just keep your cheap, $5.95 watchband. I left in a huff, only to notice there were three lights on and not a soul in any of those checkout counters. Figures!

After a brief lunch at the Airport Restaurant, reflecting on my morning happenings, I felt like a dunce. I really wasn't in all that much of a hurry. It is Monday, my usual day off. Why the fuss? Why the intemperate behavior? Sheepishly, I returned to K-Mart. Went to the jewelry counter. She was still there. I apologized for my fuming. I picked out the band I wanted, paid for it and then she said, "Let me see your watch." I misread her before. She did not have the look of a 'minimum wage employee' but the look of an angel. Calmly, quickly, she took the worn band off and put the new one on, in about a minute. "One day, a lady came in here, wanted us to put on a new band. In our attempt, it fell on the floor and broke. The company was liable. You understand the policy, don't you?" "Yes, ma'am." I told her that my experience at K-Mart today was an exercise in patience. "Our pastor preached on patience last Sunday and told us that we ought not be too surprised how we can best learn that," she said. I told her I have been working on it for fifty years. And I thanked her for the fine sermon she had just preached. On my way out, I caught the eye of the manager. We smiled at each other. He invited me to come back. Probably will, for you never know where a good sermon might show up.

October 18, 2004

Sound and Silence

Many mornings I go to the Airport Restaurant for breakfast. This past Saturday I got there early, about 6 A.M. and found I had the back room to myself. I sat in the back corner, all by myself. Alone. Time to do a little reading. Kind of like sanctuary. Quiet time. I had my sermon notes and newspaper (they often go hand in hand). I thought "This is great—maybe I can have the room to myself." The waitress kept bringing me the coffee and I kept indulging myself with the libation while cogitating on not-so-earthly stuff. It wasn't long until the room was filled. My need for a silent place was betrayed by sounds, all kinds of sounds that made serious thinking impossible. Of course, the restaurant is open for business and they weren't renting out office space for crafting sermons.

It wasn't long until I started listening to the content of those sounds. I heard a heated conversation over the fact that regular gas was $1.95 a gallon. Another group were comparing illnesses and doctor visits, and of course, you never go very far in North Carolina but what people are obsessed to a frenzied degree about

Nascar. A mother was sharing about a strained relationship with her daughter, while a father was getting an update about the grade cards that had just come out. There was another conversation about the scarcity of flu shots. Ever wonder why people talk so loud? You get the feeling that they want to let you in on the details, or they are so oblivious to their surroundings that even to a not-so-interested listener can't help but be an inactive participant. In that one hour I got a 'full plate' and for someone who just wanted coffee, I got my fill!

Then I got to thinking about what I had been through in the past week. The contacts and the chaos that go with the turf of ministry are never neat and nicely scheduled. A couple came by to talk about their marital problems. Another wanted to talk about financial problems and wondered where he could get help. A call came, asking for food and some assistance on the rent. A core of dedicated men showed up to wash windows. A single mother with four children wanted some money for school shoes for the winter. Clergy meetings, along with committee and pastoral obligations filled the week. I discovered that my Saturday morning coffee and day-in, day-out of ministry are not all that unrelated.

Sometimes I feel like that in ministry; that is, leave me to my silence, my desert—don't invade my space. Then, all of a sudden it gets messy. Confusing. Chaotic. Agonizingly disruptive. Waiting and eating. People smile a lot when they eat. Filling the stomach is a ritual of deep delight. I watched. Noticed the sheer delight that comes with the 'filling'. I suppose church ought to be something like that. We preachers tell them to "come and dine". And when they do come, we realize that church, at its best, is not an empty building, but a place where people come to find something to eat. And if there were time to hear all the chatter that must go in the lives of those who come, it would not be unlike what I overheard at the Airport Restaurant. It's just that my tidy and clean little image of an un-messy ministry is not an option.

I stayed long enough to watch a group eat and go, then another assembly of hungry people did the same. The waitresses clean the tables, take orders and we all go through it again. Kind of like a sermon. The joy of getting it done, delivered and over with. Then, about Wednesday, you know Sunday's coming again. There are times I love to come to the church when it is empty and I am all alone. I take the phone off the hook. I relish being uncluttered and unavailable for a while. For just a little while. For me and my inner world. But it doesn't last too long, just long enough, I suppose. I imagine a car stops. A door slams. An elderly man is walking towards the front door. He looks hungry—body and soul! I will meet him at the DOOR. I wouldn't want it any other way.

October 25, 2004

Do You Ever Wonder Where Sermons Come From?

Do you ever wonder where sermons come from? Or where an idea gets started? Most of the time I begin with Scripture, the lectionary lesson for the week. Sometimes they are launched as you 'exegete' life and that takes you to the Word. Sometimes the preacher is given a serendipity—a bonus that happens as a happy surprise. And I suppose there are more of them than we imagine because we have difficulty in reading their implied significance. Well, a strange thing that happened to me this past week. I shouldn't have been surprised, but I was. When I got to church on Tuesday morning I noticed two bags of something at the church's front door. It was two bags of clothing, stuffed in a large white plastic bag and a very much used pillow case. They contained clothing that had been stuffed in there for a couple of weeks. The smell and the looks made me take them quickly to the garbage cans. I was mystified by it all. Somewhat taken aback, I thought to myself, "We don't have a clothes closet here for the needy at the church; maybe they got the wrong church. Maybe they were yard sale leftovers and someone thought rather than throwing them away, someone at the church might be able to use them. Maybe the contributor wanted to play a joke on Pastor Chuck just to see what he would do." But I have to admit, my first response was "We don't take garbage here at the church...we have no need for unclean clothes...how brazen of someone to drop off their stuff like a sack of garbage flung to the wind and scattered along the roadside."

After some sober reflection, I started to think more wholesomely about the whole situation. These may have been 'gifts' from a well-intentioned donor with God-like motives. Then it hit me. Maybe we have analogy here! The Church and a couple of bags of soiled clothes. A strange juxtaposition. Come to think of it, as the prophet Isaiah said, "All my churchy righteousness and my self-imposed holiness are as filthy rags in God's sight."

Maybe the prophet was saying that is wasn't the clothes that smelled as much as smug, arrogant attitudes and feelings of spiritual superiority. Forgetting our own history has a way of distorting the truth. So, I was caught again—remembering the day I came to the 'door of His grace,' left there broken and worthless, like a bag of soiled, torn, and easily discardable debris. He invited me in, welcomed and embraced me into beginning again. And for nearly fifty years He has been doing a 'cleansing job' on me.

Well, I took the laundry home (and indeed some of it was beyond repair) and washed it. It all became my closing illustration for yesterday's sermon on "In the Beginning, Again and Again." I held the clean garments in my arms as the story of my own life. Getting to start over again. I told the church that we were in the process of writing a 'vision statement' of ministry for the next five years. I closed my sermon with this: "If the kingdom of God is a patchwork quilt with every conceivable shade, design and pattern—where are we in the mosaic? Whatever we come up with in our vision statement, I trust it will make clear that regardless of who, what, or where—you can begin again. Just like these newly washed garments." And indeed, before the day was over, the garments found a new home.

87

November 5, 2004

Good News

Good News comes in assorted packages…

…For this Red Sox fan whose team has languished for over fifty-five years as the underbelly of the Yankees, I call it 'good news' to come within an out, to rally to win, and then win eight games in a row to clinch the World Series. That is probably one of the greatest sporting events in a hundred years. Good news for some, bad news for others. Did you know that there are angry merchants in Boston who have been thriving on their losing—cashing in on the cash because of the 'curse'? No curse—no cash, I suppose.

…For someone who has never watched a North Carolina Tar Heels football game to its completion until the Mighty 'Canes' came to town. The game was tied until the final play, a field goal, gave the game to the Heels. I understand it was the first time in North Carolina history that they beat any team ranked in the top five. Good news to some, agony for others. Good News for a team who has been the butt of every joke of a 'wannabe' football team. Bad news for a team that will not be competing for #1 in the country this year.

While all of this was going on we were having a national election. And we sure had one! Pundits aplenty were paid good salaries to parse the nuances and blathering that made up much of the rhetoric to get my vote. I listened carefully. I can honestly say that I was one of the uncommitted until the last day. As my friend Jim Harnish (Pastor at Hyde Park United Methodist Church, Tampa) said, "We all had an election hang-over. A hang-over of victory and a hang-over of defeat." You don't get over this kind of a hangover with a couple of aspirins and orange juice. The very fiber of our nation is being tested. We cannot continue to inebriate our sensibilities with an intoxicating elixir of arrogance and pride that both parties have imbibed in, leaving behind the carnage of what self-interest and self-indulgence have produced. Yet, the electorate has spoken. The direction-arrow has been set. The acid test for both sides is how we are going to move ahead, together. I am weary of the country being labeled 'red and blue' states, that much of the nation is called the 'fly-over' section. But we are divided, deeply divided. Some would say, "Good news for some, bad news for others." If that is all we get out of this four-year cycle of endless posturing and preening, then may God have mercy on us! The 'hangovers' will continue to get worse and our demise certain. Not unless, of course, we come to see that we are the 'red, white, and blue' and the white stands for cleansing.

Cleansing! After the celebration, shouting and jubilation over whatever. The Red Sox Nation emerges; the Tar Heels take 'front and center', at least for a moment, from the Blue Devils; and the Republicans take joy in being saddled with an incredible possibility—life goes on! But there is another kind of ecstasy, an inner shouting of the sort that would cause even the Red Sox Nation to blush and any political foray to pale into insignificance. This Sunday, five individuals are going to be baptized at the church—three adults and two children, all new believers. Good news, for them and for the church. It will all happen very quietly in the little town of Mayodan, no glaring headlines, no front-page publicity. It will be a small statement about cleansing. They are choosing to go in another direction, a new path, a new life, a new way of 'doing' life. Two sets of parents, offering their infants for baptism, will be taking vows on the children's behalf and the congregation will take their vows, too. Kingdom work, sometimes hurtful, hefty and hardy; other times freighted with mind-boggling and heart warming illustrations of 'cleansing'. Baseball, politics, sports…While I wait patiently for another Indiana Hoosier National Basketball Championship, none of this even comes close to what is going to occur on Sunday morning in the little town of Mayodan at the United Methodist Church.

November 10, 2004

I Could Have Danced All Night

I am still reeling from a most incredible weekend of ministry in my life. It was not the stuff that makes for a best-selling novel, nor would it get headlined in the best newspapers. Some things just happen and when they are over you look back and realize you just traversed over holy ground. Well, it went something like this…Last Saturday evening the church had what we called "The $1000 Gala," a debt-reduction event for the church. Individuals purchased tables and decorated them with their best china and silverware and invited friends to join them in celebrating a catered gourmet meal that would rival anything you would find at a pricey restaurant. Following the meal, we went into the sanctuary where we were thrilled and entertained by tenor extraordinaire, Anthony Hearn, which was like bringing the Metropolitan Opera to the town of Mayodan. It was the kind of an evening when ones soul danced; in fact, dancing would have been so appropriate! A visitor stopped by my office today and said of it, "I never dreamed we would ever experience something like that in Mayodan." The church was nearly packed and we all left with a sense of 'arriving' at a place that went well beyond "a paper plate and plastic spoon" approach to life. Then there was cleanup. I got home around 11 P.M. knowing full well that Sunday was coming.

Sunday. It happens 52 times a year. Often routine. Sometimes 'going through the motions'. On rare occasions, 'ah ha'. More times than not, 'ho hum'. Saturday night, exhausted, I collapsed into bed but was so keyed-up I couldn't sleep. At five in the morning I was back in my office, shuffling papers and trying to put my best 'take' on the sermon. But there was something else brewing—we would be celebrating the two sacraments: baptism and the eucharist. And 'lo and behold' that ended up being the sermon. Chasity and Sam, and their son, Chase, were baptized. Lucy Dawn and her father were also baptized (Kela had already been baptized). Two young couples, barely beyond their teens, were saying 'yes' to believer's baptism. I had been working with them for some time. They were ready to make some choices that would point them in a direction they had never taken before. They wanted to have a fresh faith in a way that would assist them in building firmer foundations. When the parents—John, Sam, and Chasity—knelt at the altar, they asked forgiveness in repentance, and in the ritual of the baptism they became identified as Christian believers and members of Christ's Holy Church. It was quite a scene. When I held Chase and Lucy Dawn in my arms, made the sign of the cross on their foreheads, baptized them 'in the Name of the Father, Son, and Holy Ghost', a mystery happened. They also became members of the Church of Jesus Christ. The seal of God's grace and the benediction of His love will always be upon them. They will never, ever be un-baptized. They belong to God! Many family members and supporting friends surrounded them at the altar. The entire church entered into covenant with them, pledging their prayers and support. When that happened, the family of God got just a little big bigger!

Then came the sermon. It was brief. The sermon had already been preached. I spoke briefly about "fresh starts and second chances!" The sermon already had its illustration. All I had to do was point to the sacred elements: bread and wine! For in them are the ingredients necessary for anyone wanting 'a fresh start or a second chance'. All the 175 people came forward to the table—they pulled up a chair for He said, "Come and dine." There was plenty to eat and to drink. And we left with plenty and to spare. The benediction was given and the people dispersed. And I have been dancing ever since. Frankly, "I could have danced all night, I could have danced all night and still have begged for more. I could have spread my wings and done a thousand things I'd never done before; I'll never know what made it so exciting; why all at once my heart took flight, I only know when He began to dance with me, I could have danced, danced, danced all night." (From the musical "My Fair Lady")

Dancing. "I never dreamed we would ever experience something like this in Mayodan," someone said. Me, either. Our Lord is always welcoming new dancing partners. It is happening in Mayodan and anywhere else you might be. Shall we dance? I guess I should not be all that surprised by what happened this past weekend. Mystery is all around us. We just need to 'taste and see' that the Lord is good! And the GOOD tastes a lot like break and wine. "I will lead you in the dance," said He. I was given a gift. Again. That it is all about Him. That is why the Kingdom has five new dancers: Sam, Chasity, Chase, John and Lucy Dawn.

November 23, 2004

Pastor...Pastus...Pascere

For seven months, I have been preaching the lectionary lessons from the prophets—Isaiah, Hosea, Amos, Joel, Habbakuk and Jeremiah. Those old boys never gave you a break and never let up. They got messages from God and spewed them forth without hesitation, sometimes lacing their preachments with venom-like ferocity that indicated they were not interested in currying favor with the populace. It didn't make all that much difference whether the Israelites were looking at the consequences of going into exile, of being in exile, or coming out of exile—their pattern seemed to be predictable: obedience, transgression, judgment and return. Through it all we caught a glimpse of the major themes: that there are consequences to choices, that God's justice must be meted out, that He would not tolerate disobedience, and that in spite of their waywardness, grace always seemed to be present.

Yesterday's pericope was Jeremiah 23:1-6. The theme shifted. This time the prophet was talking to those in positions of leadership. He calls them 'pastors' (King James). RSV uses the word 'shepherd'. At any rate, the prophet tells them God is going to hold them responsible with judgment for their fraudulent dereliction of duty. Jeremiah uses the imagery and analogy of the shepherd as the one who is to take care of those under his control. And if he violates that trust, he will pay the scathing consequences. In Dante's *Inferno*, hell burns hottest for the hypocrites, for those who say one thing and do something else, for those who betray the trust in order to satisfy their own need for aggrandizement. The prophet Jeremiah had me in mind when he wrote those words long ago; maybe Dante, too.

There was a moment in my sermon when I was caught off guard. I mentioned my ordination back in 1969, when Bishop Mueller laid his hands upon my head and said, "Charles Killian, take thou the authority to be an elder in the church, to preach the Word and administer the sacraments." When I said those words, I was overcome with emotion and had one of those long pauses in which to gain my composure. Could it have been that in some small measure 'apostolic succession' became more real to me at that moment that I had ever realized? The Bishop had written 2 Tim. 2:15 on the inside cover of my presentation Bible. "Study to show thyself approved into God, a workman that needeth not to be ashamed, rightly dividing the word of truth." That verse still haunts me. I looked out at my congregation and confessed that I was given an awesome task, being pastor of the Mayodan flock. And I laid out some of my convictions about ministry and preaching along with my priorities that would chart our course in the days ahead.

What I didn't share was this—When I was a senior in seminary, prior to being launched into ministry, a group of us students invited Bishop Arthur G. Moore, one of the greatest bishops in the Methodist Church, to my apartment. We had refreshments and then we settled down for business. I opened the conversation with this 'sage of a man' and said, "Bishop, we are about to graduate and go out into the ministry. Tell us, give us three things we need to do in order to be successful in the ministry." I thought it was a good question. There was a long pause. He looked at me, rather penetratingly, and said, (slowly) "Love people…love people…love people." We young eager theologians had paper and pen ready to write, but when he responded as he did, we were rather dumbfounded. Another long pause. And, of course, I had to break the silence. "Yeah, yeah, we know that. Now, tell us what three things we need to know in order to be successful in the ministry." More awkward pausing. "Gentlemen," he said, "I wouldn't be surprised but what that just might be your problem. Think about it." And we did think about it.

And I have been thinking about it for forty years. And here I am, in Mayodan doing my level-best, loving people. And you know what? There is no better definition of 'pastor' than *loving people*. Jane and I feel fortunate indeed that we get to do this 'loving' in such a loving place.

This past Sunday in our "Celebrating the Harvest" offering, when dedicated people and their sacrificial giving netted $29,404 towards indebtedness. That will pay off one mortgage note, leaving about $15, 000 for capital improvements and the establishment of a Parsonage Building Fund. Friends, this 'offering-statement' is more than money. In less than three years, the Mayodan United Methodist Church erased a debt of $172,000. We scaled what some thought was an unscalable mountain. We sailed victoriously over troubled waters that many thought would be our doom. The shackles of a 'dark time' in our history have been reduced to dust. Phoenix-like, we have risen out of the ashes to soar again as Isaiah said, "They that wait upon the Lord shall renew their strength; they shall walk and not faint." We will continue to wait on the Lord! As we move together into the tomorrows, pastor and parish, clergy and congregation alike, we are going to "love people…love people…love people" and leave the rest up to God!

December 7, 2004

Advent Thoughts

Advent Thought #1 A hunter was walking along the road in the mountains of New Mexico and came upon a legendary hunting guide lying on the road with his ear to the ground. The hunter went over and listened. The guide said, "Large wheels, Ford pickup truck, green color, man driving with large hunting dog in back, Colorado license plate and traveling about 40 miles an hour." The hunter was astounded. "You mean to tell me that you can tell all that just by listening with your ear to the ground?" "Ear to the ground, nothing," the famed hunting guide said, "That was the truck that just ran over me."

Before you get run over by the holiday season again, it might be best to 'put your ear to the ground' and listen for the still, small sounds of this sacred time of the year. At Mayodan United Methodist Church you will hear some of those sounds. It happens every Sunday morning about 11:00.

Advent Thought #2   I learned to play chess from an expert, one of those guys who even plays the game by the mail. He won every game. One time, however, I thought I was doing better and was going to checkmate him, but I soon realized I was losing again. So I turned the board around and said, "What would you do if you were in my place?" "Well," he said, "you cannot win." Then he explained how, about 12 moves earlier, I had fallen into a trap he had set. I was defeated way back at the start—before I even knew it. The moves one makes at the beginning of Advent will determine whether one wins this Christmas or not. Often we get trapped right at the beginning of the season and don't realize it until it is too late. We are getting ready for Christmas at the Mayodan United Methodist Church, and we talk about things like that around 11:00 every Sunday morning.

Advent Thought #3   I have a friend who says that the only problem with sunrise is that it comes up so early in the morning. Maybe that friend is right! With change of the seasons you don't have to get up quite so early to experience the best free show in town: to feel the freshness of the morning air, to see the red-orange glow of the rising sun breaking through the puffy, white layers of clouds. It's a great show. Too bad so many of us miss it because it comes so early in the morning. Across church history one of the most common images of the coming of Christ in our experience is the image of light breaking into the darkness, the sun rising over the earth bringing new life and new hope. Advent is the season when Christian people face up to the reality of the darkness in their lives and in our world. But it is also the season which is filled with hope as we anticipate the rising of the Son, the coming of Christ. We talk about things like this at the Mayodan United Methodist Church. Check it out!

Advent Thought #4 The Advent of Jesus Christ is the hinge of history. All that went before, and all that comes after, pivot around that momentous event. Malcolm Muggeridge wrote, "The coming of Jesus into the world is the most important event in human history." C.S. Lewis said, "The central miracle asserted by Christians is the Incarnation. God became man. Every other miracle prepares for this, or results from this." The manger of Bethlehem is the marvel of the ages. Think of it—God in a cradle! The hands of God which tumbled galaxies into space, became the small hands of an infant. The Advent of Christ was God's unspeakable gift of love to the world. He was the God who descended the steps of glory that we night ascend with Him to worlds unknown. At the Mayodan United Methodist Church we celebrate this colossal event that towers sublimely above all others of history. See you in church Sunday.

Advent Thought #5 Are we there yet? Children have a way of asking that question before you get out of town on your way to a vacation. And they will ask it repeatedly. Are we there yet, God? I mean, as we travel this Advent journey to the Christ, I wonder, once we get there will we be so fatigued that we won't have any time or energy left to assess whether or not we are closer to the fulfillment of his Kingdom? Will we be nearer to the place where 'the valleys will be exalted and the mountains made low, the rough places plain and the crooked straight, and the glory of the Lord revealed'? Are we within earshot of the promise of 'peace on earth and good will to all people'? Really? Are we there yet, God? (Thanks to Jim Harnish for this Advent thought)

Join us at the Mayodan United Methodist Church as we make our journey through Advent. I happens about 11:00 every Sunday morning.

December 15, 2004

What a Weekend!

What a weekend, indeed! The English language is sometimes inadequate to express the full impact of what you see, hear, feel, and experience. Like the feeling of holding your newborn baby for the first time; of gazing upon the grandeur of the Grand Canyon; or after reading about Michelangelo's great sculpture, *David*, one day you are standing alongside it and marveling; and of course, your first date, first kiss, first love. Well, I have been putting off writing about last weekend's events out of fear that if I tried to explain and describe it I might betray it. Well, what words shall we use? Awesome? Incredible? Stupendous?

Who will ever forget the "soul and the song" that the Madison Circuit Charge Choir gave us in concert? How shall we describe the excitement of the gathering congregation on Sunday morning, knowing full well we were on the edge of a mighty day in the life of the Mayodan United Methodist Church? What words could one use to sense the 'pageantry and passion' of another one of Arnetta's stem-winding sermons? Would one ever fail to remember Don Stilwell's timely words, fittingly spoken, about the journey the church has made in recent years? Even though the Bishop was without voice, his presence at our worship and his closing Prayer of Consecration, along with his radiant smile and warm congratulations, made us all feel proud that we are a part of a church bigger than ourselves.

Then came the 'burning of the mortgage'. But it was more than that; it was a 'rite of passage' for the church, a hinge on a door opening us to new horizons and adventures in faith; it was saying goodbye to a 'dark and troubling' time; it was greeting the tomorrows with resolve and resilience. Again, what words could we use to put all of this into some perspective that makes sense and at the same time, states it adequately? If you missed the weekend, you missed it. You just had to be there. Any attempts to describe a 'non-repeatable' event will fall short. I suppose the shepherds long ago said as much. Can you imagine their going home after all they had experienced and then someone asked them to describe it? That night choir and the heavenly host, along with the trip to Bethlehem, were just about more than they could handle. We are not quite sure what they said and how they said it, but they made an attempt at it. And when they finished, the crowd was 'astonished' by it all. It was like their saying: "You just had to be there."

That's the way it is with Christmas. Real Christmas. We nod in the direction of Bethlehem but the trip to the 'heart of it all' is taxing and troubling, because, if you go there, you will never be the same again. Oh, I can preach about it, prod you into believing it, and describe the event as best I can—but you just have to go there yourself. I wonder, once the Season is over, that if I asked you to describe the last two weeks in December, what words you would use? Exhausted? Irritated? Glad it is over? Won't have to endure this again for 365 days? Depressed and despondent? Broke? On and on, I suppose. Well, if this is all you can come up with, then you never even got close to Bethlehem. Don't miss going. It is still there for us all to 'go and see this thing that has happened'. You just have to be there! There is no other way around it—you just have to go there yourself! And the rest will be a part of the 'greatest story ever told'.

January 3, 2005

What a Difference a Day Makes

What a difference a day makes? We have just celebrated Christmas with our singing, our advent adorations, and our gift-giving. The Bethlehem Blessing—our Emmanuel—the 'hinge of history' event shall always be marked as the 'Day of all Days'. What a difference a day makes. Yet, on our way out of Bethlehem a little over a week ago, on our way to Epiphany where the wise men came from afar to pay homage, we had another day—a day that will live in our memories, etched on our consciousness forever. The day after Christmas the tsunami hit the Pacific Rim with a vengeance. Two incredible days: one in which the Earth was shaken by the Good News that the 'light has dawned' upon us and we will never be the same again; and another day in which the earth quaked, numbing us into a realization of our human fragility and nature's wrath. What happens when these two days collide? When Truth and trauma are 'having it out' with each other? It is the kind of mix that creates all kinds of questions about shock-and-awe tragedy alongside a just and loving God.

I have already heard it, haven't you, the question about the existence of a loving God in the midst of such carnage? There are those who are constructing scenarios that suggest it is impossible to believe in a God who exists, much less one who is touched with compassion when a tsunami crashes upon the shores of ten nations, leaving thousands upon thousands dead, most of whom were children. Horrid scenes and horrid messages are coming in that leave the most hardened shaking their heads in disbelief. The easy-answer-philosopher and the simplistic theologian, always trying to make sense out of the indescribable, have failed us with the hollow words. So the question is still asked: Where is God? Can a loving and just God permit such a travesty? "No!" they shout. And the debate continues, without solace or benefit to anyone.

I can tell you that they could make a good case for an absent God if the following were true: that is, if there were no one stopping to help; if none risked their own lives to save someone else; if no countries, communities, cities, and churches rushed to provide aid; if no dollars were pledged; if no relief agencies sprang into action; if none acted in the name of their God to offer help, aid, and prayers. If you could see that, then tell me there is no God and I will agree with you! How can you explain that which is arising all over the world? Nations from all over the globe, along with people of faith and those with none, are mobilizing the most monumental response to this natural and human catastrophe. The hearts of millions worldwide are filled with a 'God-friendly impulse' that is reaching out and suffering.

The point is that in the present crisis, as one has put it, "We're responding to the tsunami with a 'faith tsunami' of our own, a tidal wave of love and compassion that will sweep across the bodies, if not the souls, of millions affected by this disaster." A 'faith-tsunami'! Interesting! We observed Holy Communion yesterday. I put it rather crudely, I suppose. Pointing to the sacraments, I said something to the effect these are the evidences of the greatest tsunami that ever occurred. Can one truly fathom the enormity of what the condescension and humiliation of "God becoming Man" involved? All of creation, 'on the skids' by our rebellion and pride, was subsumed in the Christ, who was "touched with our infirmities." (Isaiah 53:4) God did not do an end run around our circumstances. He did not suspend tragedy for His own Son. He bore our weakness, our limitations. He walked in our shoes, he wept over our predicament. He made a way, a provision through the Incarnation, which, I believe, is another way of saying that God weeps with us! Listen to God weep and you will conclude that earthquakes and tsunamis contribute nothing to the "Does God Exist" question. Listen to God weep and the 'faith-tsunami' will continue to grow and multiply into healing and restoration because the God-instincts within us all will reach out to the suffering. And because of that, yes, Truth and Trauma will continue to fight it out. But the outcome is certain. What a difference a day makes!

January 12, 2005

Rubee

I have a suspicion that today, January 12, will be long remembered as the day we said goodbye to Rubee Sechrist. But how do you say 'goodbye' to that which will never go away? How do you bid farewell to something that is etched on your soul like chiseled stone? How do you begin to move ahead when you sense something rare and precious left you behind? In a one-hour memorial service today we attempted, inadequately, to put into words the story of the life and ministry of one about whom volumes could have been written.

Every once in awhile a pastor gets the privilege of conducting a funeral for one who has already written the sermon. Sometimes there is so much to be said, that the less you say the better. Ruby's life-long influence was the sermon. Her life had a thousand points of light, well-documented in lives of those near and far who came under the sway and power of her quiet sainthood. What more needed to be said? Well, we gathered and had our feeble say. Thanks to son, Jimmy, and granddaughter, Vickie, we were treated to a deeper glimpse of Rubee—Her innate sense of goodness, a healthy sense of humor, an unshakeable trust in Christ, a devoted love for family and friends, and a healthy respect for human dignity. I got the feeling that this person who rarely left Rockingham County has monuments erected to her honor all over the world. It'll take a lifetime or two to get through all that. I guess we can't really say 'goodbye,' can we? Nor should we! We can talk about the legacy she left us (and that is immense), but rather we should contemplate how we can best pay tribute to her memory—and you can't do that by saying 'goodbye.' If you wish to pick up the 'Rubee Mantle' you will end up being indissolubly linked to Jesus Christ with an unmovable anchor in that which is forever. So, I look around and see the imprints of her gentle and gracious hand; listening carefully I can hear pleasant and quiet assurance coming from her wisdom; and watching ever so closely I get a fresh and vivid portrait of the Christ. I don't ever want to say 'goodbye' to that!

Maybe January 12 will be long-remembered as a day when someone refused to say 'goodbye' but instead greeted it with 'hello.' Like, "Hello Rubee, I am going to start reading one of your books—your book of life, of living and loving." If you do, when you come to the 'final chapter', you will have enough to write your own sermon. Make it easy on the pastor who has to put it all together in a one-hour service. Thanks, Rubee, for having been in my life. I will see you around.

February 6, 2005

You Can't Beat those Old Songs

The discipline of writing is like any other discipline; if you don't stay at it, it will fade and falter. Much has happened since I last wrote about the tsunami. I suppose in the press of things one can think that other demands have priority and can get used to not doing it. Take faithful church attendance—it astounds me how Christian believers, who have taken the vows of church membership, can be so cavalier about that commitment; that is, if something else comes along that asks for our time, it is amazing how often 'church attendance' comes in second place. It is true of any discipline. Exercising? We all know if you aren't intentional about it and stay with it, soon it occupies less and less of your time and attention. Well, pastoring goes through the same cycle. Of all the sundry duties of pastoral care, (one of which is to call on the sick, infirm, and shut-ins), if you don't keep it on the 'must do' list, it too can easily be discarded and considered not as important as we once thought. So, in getting back to my writing, I have chosen to briefly report on what happened today at Britthaven Nursing Home. I had made about seven or eight brief visits, read some scripture and had prayers. And everyone is so appreciative of some company. Even one lady told me that she was looking forward to moving from her single room to where she would have a roommate because she wanted someone to talk to. My last visit was with Agnes Vernon and Lena Gann. Roommates, both Moravians, both grew up together in the same town, and both have each other to talk to, or to be silent with.

It wasn't very long until we got around to talking about the faith journey. Finally, Agnes said, "We had a couple of aides working in here and they got to complaining about things, so we invited them to come into our room because we had something for them. We sang for them." I asked, "What did you sing?" They said I probably didn't know the song, but the two of them began singing and soon I joined in. We sang together, "Count Your Blessings". When we finished our scratchy rendition, we all agreed that if you started counting blessings, it would eliminate a lot of grumbling. Well, one song led to another so we ended up having a songfest, much to the delight of several in the hall. We sang, "Kneel at the Cross," "Bringing in the Sheaves," "The Haven of Rest," and "Life is Like a Mountain Railroad"—songs that didn't make the last hymnal revision. When we finished our unrehearsed concert, Lena said, "You just can't beat those old songs." And I suppose she is right. Some songs had 'keeping power' for those who sang them. They were sustained and comforted by the truths they contained. In our worship this morning we sang a couple of the oldies—"Come Thou Fount of Every Blessing" and "I am Thine O Lord." Ricky Sechrist mentioned to me this evening that he thought the congregation sang better then usual this morning. I agreed. Could it be those old songs are more familiar because we have taken ownership of them, because they are a part of our religious history? Maybe that is what Lena was trying to say to me. When you get nearer to the 'end of the road', you remember and in remembering you are blessed. In spite of her infirm condition, she was counting her blessings, naming them one by one. If a song can get you to do that, then she is right: YOU CAN'T BEAT THOSE OLD SONGS.

February 15, 2005

Dying Ember

Last Sunday I gave my congregation a brief treatise on a couple of disciplines for Christian living, growing out of the passage from Matthew 4, 'the temptations of Jesus'. Prior to this episode we have the event of his baptism, in which the Voice from heaven declared, "This is my beloved son, in whom I am well pleased." Right on the heels of that incredible pronouncement, and right before the inauguration of his ministry, he is led into the wilderness where he prays for 40 days and nights, and is tempted by the devil. How did he get through it? He didn't pray to the angels or even to God to deliver him from the temptations, but he did possess a strategy and had it down cold—PRAYER AND THE WORD OF GOD. In each of the devil's suggestions, he responded, "It is written." We preachers talk a lot about these two disciplines, largely because, I think, we keep stumbling over them. Prayer and the Bible. I recall many sermons in my younger days, where preachers admonished long and hard about your prayer life and 'hiding away in your heart' the sacred Word.

Well, there was another discipline of 'church attendance.' Not going to church on Sunday was scandalous, mother would say. She told me that aside from the month we all were quarantined for scarlet fever and illness, I never missed church until I graduated from high school. While I chafed at it more times than I would like to admit, the discipline stuck. And even to this day, on vacation or whatever takes me away from my home church, there looms in the back of my mind and at the citadel of my heart: ON SUNDAYS YOU GO TO CHURCH! I suppose one of the more frustrating things I deal with in my own spirit is the cavalier attitude that so many church members who took the vow of church membership to be faithful in attendance, dismiss church attendance as something of an 'add-on', with a take-it-or-leave-it kind of attitude. I don't know where I heard it, but there is this story about the 'Dying Ember.'

A member of a certain church, who previously had been attending services regularly, stopped going. After a few weeks, the pastor decided to visit him. It was a chilly evening. The pastor found the man at home alone, sitting before a blazing fire. Guessing the reason for the pastor's visit, the man welcomed him, led him to a big chair near the fireplace and waited. The pastor made himself comfortable but said nothing. In the grave silence, he contemplated the play of the flames around the burning logs. After some minutes, the pastor took the fire tongs, carefully picked up a brightly burning ember and placed it to one side of the hearth all alone. Then he sat back in his chair, still silent. The host watched all this in quiet fascination. As one lone ember's flame diminished, there was a momentary glow and then its fire was no more. Soon it was cold and 'dead as a doornail'. Not a word had been spoken since the initial greeting. Just before the pastor was ready to leave, he picked up the cold, dead ember and placed it back in the middle of the fire. Immediately it began to glow once more with the light and warmth of the burning coals around it. As the pastor reached the door to leave, his host said, "Thanks you so much for your visit and especially for the fiery sermon. I shall be back in church next Sunday."

I reckon if all the 'embers' in the Mayodan United Methodist Church were 'aflame', we'd have a seating problem on Sunday morning. Well, there you have it…Prayer, the Word, Church Attendance. Put them all together and we all of us will light a fire that shall never go out.

February 22, 2005

I'm Just about the Richest Person in the World

"I'm just about the richest person in the world." That is what Grandma told me a long time ago. I remember where it was that she told me that. She was out spading her garden; yes, spading. It just didn't seem right for my aged grandmother to be doing that. It was hot and dirty work. "It sure would be nice, Grandma, if you had a tractor to do this work. You shouldn't have to do this," I offered. She leaned on the shovel handle, looked me in the eyes, and said, "That sort of equipment costs lots of money, something we don't have much of; on the other hand, I am just about the richest person in the world." She paused for a while and then went back to turning the sandy soil. "Rich," I bellowed, "you call this rich? You live in a two-room house with an outside toilet. You make your own soap, you darn your own socks. You take in washing and ironing to earn grocery money. You even save tin foil from a piece of gum and wouldn't think of throwing away a piece of string. Rich? We ain't rich, we're dirt poor." Grandma had heard enough. She placed the shovel against a rusty fence and sat down under a gnarly apple tree and talked to her grandson, the kind of way you knew something awesome was about to be said. "Look at the garden, Charlie. I will soon have it tilled and planted, probably by tomorrow evening. I pray that the rain will come and bless the seeds. Then, one of these days, those seeds will break through the soil and green beans will be well on their way. Why, in no time, son, we will have green beans for supper. Some corn, too. If we are lucky, some squash. Do you ever think about that? And it all gets started by turning the soil. Don't you see—we are rich? Riches are not determined by how much money you have." With that she stopped, took her spade and continued her work, knowing full well that it wouldn't be long until green beans would be cooking in the kitchen.

Well, summer came and so did the green beans, corn, and squash aplenty. One day I rode my bicycle out to see my grandparents and Grandma was in the garden, gathering her vegetables in a bushel basket. There were more than they could eat. So, the neighbors got in on the bountiful harvest. She made her way around the neighborhood, parceling out her produce, without ever asking for a cent; after all, she was the richest woman in the world and she could do that.

Well, the years came and went….all too soon. It all seems like it happened yesterday. When grandma was buried, it was done with borrowed money. When household effects were sold at auction, it barely covered the expenses. I suppose there are those who are banking on a hefty inheritance from the forbearers—and we got ours, too. A sizeable and sustainable inheritance it was! Every now and then, reflecting on my legacy, I can see Grandmother, stooped with years and with shovel in hand, getting ready for another planting as if she were making a statement to God: "I am so delighted to participate with you, God, in the making of green beans." Grandma was right, <u>money has very little to do with riches</u>! And when I get to thinking otherwise, I remember "…just about the richest person in the world."

February 27, 2005

I'm Just about the Richest Person in the World, Part II

On Sunday mornings, Grandma and Grandpa would stop by our house and take us four Killian kids to church at the Blissville Church of the Brethren. It was at that church that I was first made aware of God, in Wilda Bottorft's Sunday school class. I took my nickel, always a nickel, to her class and we were given two options for our offering. We could deposit it in a church-shaped bank and that money went to the local church. The second option was a small, round world globe. That money went for missions. I always put my nickel in the globe, and I suppose that is one of the reasons why my ministry, even to this day, has always focused on missions.

After Sunday school it was worship time. And I don't recall much of that, except that the pastor (we called him Brother Joseph) was tall and lanky and wore a clerical collar. He appeared so stately and God-like. In fact, I thought he was God—calm, kind, and a tad austere. I don't remember much about the services except the singing and the offering. The song we sang most often was "The Church in the Wildwood." You remember it, don't you… "There's a church in the valley by the wildwood, no lovelier spot in the dale; no place is so dear to my childhood, as the little brown church in the vale." Then the chorus which was Grandpa's part. His bass voice would ring out, "Oh, come, come, come, come…" all the way to the end of the chorus. The way they sang that song and the way Brother Joseph conducted himself gave me the impression that something serious was going on. I often sat next to Grandma and as we sang and listened to the scriptures being read, she would run her index finger along the lines so that I could keep up. <u>It was my first reading</u> lesson. I noticed those fingers and those hands—worn and cracked, weathered by too much use of the shovel. At offering time, she opened her purse, a shiny black patent purse. She would get out her small brown leather coin purse with metal snaps that made a loud noise when you closed it. She took a few coins out, carefully counted them, and placed them in the offering plate as it passed. She always seemed to be smiling when she did that. She would look at me and say, "My tithe for God." I had no idea what she was talking about. I did learn years later that those few coins were well beyond her ten percent. Grandma never got any social security; she got what they called 'old age pension' which amounted to less than $50 a month. And she called herself 'just about the richest woman in the world'?

I look back with fondest memory of those days, when small seeds were planted, unbeknownst to me, which eventually bloomed and <u>blossomed into a discipline</u> that to this day I have never been able to shake, 'my tithe for God'. My inheritance from the 'richest woman in the world' is <u>still bearing</u> fruit. That nickel offering is still paying dividends.

March 6, 2005

I'm Just about the Richest Person in the World, Part III

Grandmother would have made a good United Methodist even though she thought I was getting a little too liberal when I told her I joined the United Methodist Church. For one thing, she took her vows of membership seriously. When one joins the United Methodist Church, we vow to be faithful to the church by praying for the church, attending the church, offering services to the church and giving to the church. In previous mailings, I wrote about her attending, probably never missing more than a half dozen Sundays in over fifty years. She and Grandpa were there every Sunday, sitting in the same creaky pew. I wrote about her giving her 'tithe to God' she called it, which was little more than a dollar in change. Her service to the church was given to the Ladies Aid Society, which was a weekly gathering of ladies who quilted and sold their products to raise money for missions.

In 1944 (Grandma embroidered it on the quilt), she asked me what backing I would like on my quilt. I told her red. And sure enough, two weeks later, I got a quilt, with my name embroidered on it, too. I was warmed by that quilt in more ways than one. But what I remember most about grandma was her praying—the ritual and the content of it. Each evening she would kneel down by the rocker with me at her side, cover our heads with a blanket (Grandma always covered her head when she prayed and never went to church without her net prayer bonnet covering her head). She always prayed a special blessing on me, that God would protect and guide me, and that I would grow up with a heart after God. Then she prayed 'around the world,' praying for the missionaries, the hungry and the homeless, the disenfranchised and the poor. It took us awhile to get through the prayer because she went around a couple of times. What stands out in my memory is the blanket covering me. I thought it was a tent, and that Grandma and I were camping out around her old rocker, a rocker that I still sit in and 'rock and remember.' I asked her once about the 'covering' on her head and the blanket. She didn't know much about the theology of it or care very much about that except, she said, when we pray we are in the presence of God. "It is our way of showing reverence," she'd say. Grandma reverenced God. You never heard her say an unkind word about anybody. Coarse language was not in her vocabulary, each though once she said, "Darn," and we are all shocked. In spite of all her reverses, her needs, and her limited resources, she always muttered, "God is good."

I was with her in her last days. We read scripture and we prayed together. We recalled memories. We laughed and we cried. "Grandma, is there anything you would like to say to me?" knowing this just might well be my last visit. She thought for a minute and then said, "You know, Charlie, about 75 years ago, I kept quoting the first part of the 23rd Psalm. "The Lord is my shepherd; I shall not want." That was my life's verse. But in recent months I have been looking at the last part of the Psalm. "Surely goodness and mercy have followed me all the days of my life and I will dwell in the house of the Lord forever." I am as sure about that as if my soul depended on it. A few weeks later, she died. She told me something to the effect that everybody writes his own 23rd Psalm. And I am trying to focus on the end of that Psalm; trying to do my dead-level best to 'dwell in the house of the Lord forever'. It was her prayer and mine, too. If Grandma were around today, and she lived next door, I would invite her to the United Methodist Church and ask her to join. I can hear her now—'those are good vows, count on me. When do I sign up?'

March 14, 2005

10 % Chuck; 90 % Holy Spirit

My daughter, Elaine, was in the worship service yesterday. She sang and we all were blessed by the message of the song and the quality of spirit manifested in her singing. I have never heard her sing more beautifully. I think it inspired the preaching that followed. While she was singing my mind went back to thirty-five years ago when I first caught a glimpse of her imagination that started dreaming dreams at a young age, and watched her plot a future enshrined in the grace of God. She has always had the capacity to express her mind and feelings without reserve. Following the service she came into my office and gave her dad a gift that only the two of us fully fathom. Elaine has a gift of writing and when she got home last evening she wrote the piece below about her experience at Mayodan this past weekend. Her best gift to me was her take on what the percentage should look like in ministry and preaching—10% the preacher; 90 % the Holy Spirit. Come to think of it, that is just about the way to put it for anything we do.

The Lord's Day

The Lord's Day. A day set apart for remembrance. Twenty-four hours of holy rest. Time for reflection. Time for an inward pause. A day for looking into the deep things of God, the heart of God. Time belonging to Him. Moments with the Father, the Son, the Spirit. Communion with the Saints. And in the end, a word from the Sacred. Sometimes in a still, small voice. Sometimes in a gentle prod, and perhaps, sometimes in a loud voice like a trumpet.

Today was the Lord's Day, and indeed, I heard from God.

This Sunday rounded off a weekend visit to my parent's house to celebrate my mother's birthday. A trip crammed with activity, shopping, eating out, a road trip to Mt. Airy, walks around town, and movies. All activities enjoyed by mother and daughter, bonding closer in the simplicities of life. My father had to be out of town for most of the weekend, but we didn't mind. We enjoy our growing years of friendship and prize the moments of solitude we share.

Dad arrived on the scene late Saturday evening, harried by his busy weekend of teaching preachers how better to preach. After brief conversation, he scurried off to bed. He was, after all, scheduled to preach to his own congregation in a few short hours and needed the rest. We said our goodnights, and I nestled into the confines of my covers and contemplated my agenda for the next day, the Lord's Day. Would I leave early, skip church, and make it home to my busy household by lunchtime? Should I stay and worship with my folks, only to miss my afternoon nap because of the three-hour drive ahead of me? What should I do? Both good options; both easily rationalized.

I would stay, on the Lord's Day, enter into his house and into his Spirit, with the complete expectation of hearing his voice. A whisper would be fine, more than enough for my growing faith and childlike anticipation. My prayer? "Just a little more of your glory revealed today, Lord. Let me see you a little bit clearer."

From the moment I entered into Mayodan United Methodist Church, I could sense God's Spirit in the midst. He'd already arrived, long ahead of me, and I was warmed by his familiar greeting. I made my way to my dad's office, hoping to have a word with him prior to the service. He was busied by the usual chaos that often attends a pastor's Sunday morning experience. Details of the bulletin, ushers and lay leaders, last minute questions of protocol, greetings of the congregation, laughs and hugs, and in the middle of it all, a daughter wanting to love her dad a little. We commented about the busyness, the business of the morning, and I told him that no matter how fractured we might "feel," God's in the business of showing up anyway. In fact, He's already arrived.

What a privilege to feast in his presence, in God's spirit,

on this His day. From the "Greeting" to the "Benediction," God breathed, God intended, God in a whisper. All ordained from the throne room of the heavenlies, just for me, and for all of those who came expecting and dared to listen.

For almost thirty-nine years now, I've listened to the numerous "sermons" my father had preached. Some from a pulpit, some from a dinner table, some in a conversation with friends, some from a classroom. Some in walks along the path. Some from the sins called mistakes. Many from the forgiveness called grace. And while I've heard them all, perhaps I've never heard one quite like today's. God's spirit fell upon my father in full measure this morning. His words were not rehearsed. No notes to lean on. No great soliloquies to recite. Just 'raw Chuck' and the Holy Spirit working together as God has always intended for it to be. Indeed, a little piece of God's glory given to me.

When the service ended, I was overwhelmed by the many graces God allowed me to witness in the brief span of an hour. Tender to the "Things of God," I hugged my dad and told him, "That was 10 % Chuck and 90 % the Holy Spirit. Stick with the Word, Dad. He'll show up every time." Not much else could be said. I don't know my dad's take on my growing faith, sometimes bordering on a more charismatic bent. I feel a bit awkward encouraging my dad with my words of faith, but nevertheless, how can I be silent when I serve God who is called Faithful, who is faithful? (Rev. 19:11)

I asked him to meet me. I honored him with my presence that day, his Lord's Day, and I was in the Spirit. He came. He spoke. Perhaps not with the trumpet of John's revelation, but he came, tapped me on my heart, and revealed a little more of himself to me through his beloved disciple, my dad. Does it get any more blessed than that?

My earthly father revealing my heavenly Father's glory to me! Now that is something worth shouting about.

May 11, 2005

A Small Episode and the Kingdom of God

I don't know why it is so difficult for me to keep disciplined about my writing. I really enjoy doing it, but sometimes the press of duties and other 'stuff' get in the way of this part of my ministry. Maybe it is a lot like church attendance; once you get out of the habit it is hard to get back into it. Of course, I don't really know what that means because every Sunday I have to show up. While I might be doing well in that regard, other areas sometimes fall into arrears.

Well, today an individual passed my way: Danny Bowman—I met him today. There is this man who is always sitting on the Mayodan Cemetery brick wall when I pass by on my way to Madison or the Airport Restaurant. He always waves with his left hand extended in a 'shooting position', with his index finger pointing right at me. This has been going on for three years. I asked someone who he was. No one seemed to know. I said to myself, "One of these days, I am going to stop and find out his name." Today, after breakfast, I made a commitment to stop and meet him if he were on the cemetery wall. Sure enough, there he was. I stopped and we had a twenty-minute conversation. I told him how much I appreciated his always waving at me and I wanted to meet him. He invited me to sit with him and we talked. He told me his name and that he was on disability but he would be glad to mow my yard if I needed some help.

It wasn't long until I realized he was one of God's special persons. Marginalized. Poor. Handicapped. And possessing a gentle and kind spirit. The kind of a person, meek in nature, who is going to end up inheriting the world. We talked and we got around to religion. I asked him if he believed in God. He said, "If you don't believe in God you don't have very much left." Right. For Danny, who has very little, appeared to have it all. When I got ready to leave, he thanked me for stopping by and talking with him. He said that doesn't happen very often. We shook hands about six times. And he told me that I was quite a talker. Right, again. He asked me to pray for his wife, Pat. I told him I would. And I left him there on his own little chapel, waving to all the passers-by as if he knew their names. But I don't think it was my 'talking' nor my believing in God that made his day. Danny Bowman made my day. I think it was just taking twenty minutes out of an incredibly busy schedule to be alongside one of God's special persons. It reminded me once again that when you 'do it unto the least of these' you do it unto ME.

July 11, 2005

May I Have Seconds?

The last time I wrote you all, Jane and I were headed for the country of Estonia. We had a great trip and a good ministry. We have been to Estonia several times; my first venture there was in 1994 when I helped start a seminary for theological education in this former Soviet Republic. For me the highlight was to see some of my former students now actively involved in making their witness felt in that place.

I learned a rather sobering statistic on this most recent trip—only 20% of Estonians believe in God. Ministry would be like trying to carve marble with a wooden knife. Discouraging and disheartening at times, I was told. Yet while the work is difficult the ministry goes on. When I asked, "What keeps you going…keeps you at it?" They responded, "It is all about the grace of God." What do you do when you feel empty? When it seems like there is nothing left to give? When the rewards are few and far between? And as I was told by one of my former students, "There are times when you wonder if what little you do makes that much difference." Well, that is often the way it is in ministry.

When I returned home, I had a stack of mail. One letter came from Christopher Brown, a high school graduation announcement. Chris was four years old when I pastored that church in Taylorsville, Indiana. It was on a Sunday in which we were celebrating the Eucharist. At that time, I had all the children come to the altar at one time and gave them the elements. I talked about the 'bread' and 'wine' as simply as I knew how. Then I gave them a small piece of bread and the thimble full of wine. They reverently ate the bread and drank the cup. Then I heard Christopher say, "Pastor Chuck, Pastor Chuck (holding out the empty communion cup to me), may I have seconds?" He was serious. I imagine he was thirsty. Could it be that in a four-year-old's mind he was shocked by the size of that drinking glass? I noticed some in the congregation were smiling and wanted to break into laughter. Me, too. But Chris had it right! In his innocence and childlike way he was telling me certainly there is more where this came from! And indeed there is! Grace upon grace we are given; and it is that abundance that keeps them going in Estonia; and it is that grace which enables us to keep focus when we wonder sometimes if what little we give in the name of Christ makes that much difference. It is all about the grace of God, with some 'bread and wine' thrown in. Seconds, anyone?

August 8, 2005

The Price of a Memory

Much has happened since the last 'ramblings'. I fulfilled a lifelong dream of watching my favorite baseball team, the Boston Red Sox, play at Fenway Park. When I was a small lad, I couldn't wait until the South Bend Tribune arrived so that I could 'read all about it'—those baseball scores. I would check to see if my Red Sox won or lost. If they won, I had a good night's sleep; if they lost, I dreamed for a better day tomorrow. Well, this past July, I took my two oldest grandsons and we flew to Boston. We managed to ride the subway to downtown. The crowds, my sense of direction, and the massive number of cars and people were a tad overwhelming, but we made it to our motel that was within a fifteen-minute walk to the stadium. We arrived on a Monday afternoon. I had tickets for Tuesday and Wednesday, but we decided to walk to Fenway Park, and although we didn't have tickets for the Monday game, we wanted to see the park, and maybe by chance 'scalp' three tickets.

I cannot describe my feelings as I rounded Ipswich Street and saw the forbidding 'Green Monster'—the place where Ted Williams handled the ball coming off that wall, holding the batter to a single. I was a little boy again, remembering the times I played the ball off the side of Mrs. Campbell's barn and imagining I threw out the runner trying to make it to second base. With a glad heart, I was in Boston, standing under the banner that announced the 2004 World Series Champions, while the grandsons wondered if they were going to be able to see the game. There were a few scalpers and the prices were well beyond my budget. But I saw the look on the faces of my grandsons. They weren't pushing me. They knew the prices were out of reach. For a seat that was priced at $25, the asking on the street was $175, each. I told the boys that maybe closer to the game time, we might find something a little less expensive. They quietly agreed. "let's look around some more; I am sure we might strike up a better deal." They were hard to come by. "Do you have three tickets together?" I asked another seller, thinking surely there wouldn't be three seats together. "How much?" I still couldn't believe it. I bartered and begged. I finally shelled out $200 for three tickets. Wide-eyed and mouths agape, the three of us walked proudly onto the hallowed grounds of Fenway Park.

When I told my father many, many years ago about my dream to go to Boston and watch the Red Sox, he wished me well, but indicated I probably would never make it to the ball park.

Somewhere around the 7th inning, with the Red Sox leading, I had a conversation with Dad. "Well, Dad, I made it to Boston, with my Nick and Colton." And Dad replied, "You paid WHAT for those three seats?" "They are good seats, Dad." "Eight dollars for a pretzel and coke? That is almost unforgivable," he added. Then he looked into the faces of my deliriously happy grandsons and said, "I am glad you made it to Boston, Son; and if I could have been there with you, I would have picked up the whole tab." And I am confident that he would have returned to Tyner, Indiana, penniless to get it done. I returned to Mayodan, having forgotten about budgetary concerns, because I was in Boston with my grandsons, watching the Red Sox. You just can't put a price tag on a memory.

August 14, 2005

"Sunday Mornin' Coming Down"

Johnny Cash sang Kris Kristofferson's song, "Sunday Morning' Coming Down" in which he wrote about the agony and loneliness of a Sunday morning sidewalk. I, too, have had some Sunday mornings like that. Last night was not a restful night. Fits of sleep and strange dreams danced with each other throughout the night. In the dark stillness, I waited for the clock to signal my usual Sunday morning rising...5:30 A.M. Paper and coffee at 'Fuzzy's', along with an unpreached sermon stared me in the face. I go through my Sunday morning ritualistic doldrums: Why do I do what I do? Why go through this weekly turmoil? Why am I doing this to myself? Do I have anything to say worth hearing? Will it make any difference, anyway? These are the kinds of questions that rarely greet me during the week, but on Sunday morning, the sermon must show up on time, ready and waiting to be listened to. These are the kinds of questions that have been my fare for forty years. Preaching has never been a 'cake walk' for me. Even though I consistently spend 20-25 hours a week in preparation, this 'sacrament in time that gives meaning to time' (Donald Miller, *Fire In Thy Mouth*) often eludes my best intentions.

But 'Sunday morning is comin' down' and I make my way to the church, turn on the lights, and do my last bit of 'getting ready' before the gathering starts. My ritual usually consists of going into the sanctuary, sitting in the pulpit chair, standing behind the pulpit, and going through some of my thinking and planning out loud. Then I kneel at the altar and offer prayer for help, asking forgiveness for my inadequacies. And there have been occasions where there seemed to be nothing, but 'light and fire' showed up anyway. I do not understand that, other than to come to the conclusion that if God does show up later in the morning, it is His doing and not mine. The 'shock and awe' of it all still baffles me. The rigors of study and preparation haunt my feeble presentations. And when the day is over, I still end up in the 'wonder of it all'.

I suppose these questions will greet me every Sabbath morning. And out of faithfulness, I will take another stab at this thing called preaching. And as long as I still feel 'antsy and edgy' about this business I will keep doing it. Someday I am sure I will sleep soundly through Saturday nights and there will be no early conversations with God, and I won't even have any questions. That will be the day when it is all over. Finished. Until then, I will live with the agonizing dilemma that I am caught between two worlds—this one and the one to come—and I trust my preaching will respond to the question every congregation asks of its preacher, as Fred Craddock put it, "What did you find when you were in there this week?" Preaching—God's incredible, amusing and amazing sense of humor, that he would choose to use the likes of me to communicate His Word. Laughable stuff, I tell you. Laughable, to be sure. But as long as I can laugh, I will continue to endure, knowing that grace will 'show up' when Sunday morning is 'comin' down'.

September 12, 2005

Cracker-Barrel Church

A couple of weeks ago I was in Troy, IL, celebrating with United Methodists on their 200th anniversary of the beginnings of Methodism in Illinois. My housing arrangements were at the Red Roof Inn and across the street was the Cracker Barrel where I would eat most of my meals. I didn't mind that, for the Cracker Barrel has been my stopping off place for many a meal as I have traveled up and down the Interstates. You can see their signs conspicuously thrust into the skyline, announcing their whereabouts. Their reputation has followed them since their inception in 1969. You stop, eat and relax, and afterwards you feel better for the experience. And you are ready to travel on!

I got to thinking about that on Saturday morning. In fact, I hung around the 'Old Country Store' for a couple of hours. I fiddled with the mind-teaser on the table, drank several extra cups of coffee and wondered, "Where am I? Where did this all get started? What is the 'story' here about Cracker Barrel and its operations?" Finally, one of the managers, Mary Mendoza, stopped by my table to see if everything was fine and I assured her that it was. I asked about the Troy Cracker Barrel and she said she was here at its beginning. Twenty years ago "there was nothing here but a truck stop. And with the coming of three Interstates it was assumed this would be a good place for a Cracker Barrel. And it has been." I asked her, "What is the mission of Cracker Barrel? Does the management have a philosophy that governs and directs what you do?" Without hesitation, she said, "It is simple and direct: <u>Pleasing people</u>. We have two groups of people to please—internal and external, our employees and our customers. And if we do our job, both will be happy. This is all about pleasing people...that's just about it." She encouraged me to go to Crackerbarrel.com if I wanted more info.

The 'Pleasing People' motto got me thinking and I couldn't escape its simplicity and unsophisticated brevity. I rummaged around the store, examining the Halloween and Christmas displays, the sound recordings, the clothing and footwear, the books and candles, children's toys, and ended up spending an hour in one of those $129 rocking chairs at the front door. I felt so very far away from everything that I normally do; yet I felt so close to something kind of special and deep.

When I got home, I did go to Crackerbarrel.com. I discovered something of its roots, history, mission, and outreach. It sounded rather spiritual and enriching. On September 19, 1969, the first Cracker Barrel opened in Lebanon, TN. It began with Dan Evins' dream of establishing a place to better meet the needs of folks on the road. The interstate system was still young. Goods and services were sparse and often not to be trusted. While fast foods might be a good business idea, Dan felt it wasn't such a hot eating idea. He saw mealtime as something special –a time to catch up with the family, your friends, or your thoughts. Meals weren't meant to be swallowed down in three bites with a squirt of ketchup. He knew that building a country store would not be the same thing as being one. A lot of things would have to be just right, the two most important being 'what was served' and 'who was serving it'.

Well, people liked the Old Country Store and word got around. It was so successful that the company went public with its stock. In the 80's eighty-four stores opened across the country. By the mid-90's there were 260; and today there are 533 locations in 41 states. They explain their success, as Mary Mendoza told me, by pleasing people; or as Dan Evins puts it, "It is a mutual respect concept." Things are likely to stay that way, because the way Dan sees it, the lifestyle of rural America isn't about where you live, it is about how you live.

"Pleasing people. Nothing more. Nothing less." The management is convinced that if they keep doing that they have a fair chance of success. I was fascinated that they have an Outreach Department.

Since pleasing people is so central to what they value, they believe that their success is based on their ability to live out that mission statement every day. They work hard to protect and to promote that commitment; and they are so serious about that, they have established the Outreach function which evaluates, enhances, and promotes the company's commitment to inclusion for guests, employees, and vendors in order to improve company performance.

When I put all of this together, I come up with 'The Cracker-Barrel Church Model' for ministry:
1. How serious am I about dreams and visions, about how to meet the needs of wary and hungry travelers?
2. How committed am I to fostering an attitude and mood of mutual respect?
3. How do I manage my 'two groups of people'—those inside and those outside the church?
4. How concerned am I about 'what is being served' and 'who is doing the serving?'
5. How can I continue to maintain integrity with the past and keep faith with the future?
6. How do you 'dream big dreams' and still keep the vision alive that got it all started with humble beginnings?
7. How do you make the faith journey exciting, stimulating, and exhilarating, while at the same time you don't forget where you came from?
8. How do I deal with that which does not change in a world that is constantly changing?
9. How can I make the worship 'mealtime' a place where you just don't go through the motions of a fast food experience but take time to treasure the eating together?
10. How seriously do I take the 'outreach' component? As Bishop Roy Nichols once said, "The Church is the only institution that exists solely for those who do not belong."

Thanks, Cracker Barrel, for being there by the side of the road at a busy time in the busy world of this weary traveler. Something to think about! God help me to 'meet the needs of the folks on the road'.

September 25, 2005

"I'm Caught Up."

Last week I ran into someone who hasn't been to church in months. For whatever reason he felt he needed to justify his not being in church or at least to tell me something that might help me understand his lengthy absence. Even though I have never asked for any reason, I have become accustomed to a variety of statements. Here are a few I have heard:

> Sunday is my only day off. I need a day to rest and relax.
> I get to bed so late on Saturday night; I just can't get up on Sunday morning.
> I worship best out in the woods, hunting; or on the lake fishing.
> I go to the lake cottage and that is where I spend my Sabbath rest.
> I have just gotten out of the habit.
> Going to church is just one of many options I have every Sunday.
> The best TV news broadcast comes in the middle of Sunday morning, and I wouldn't miss Face the Nation for anything."

In addition, I have heard some say that the worship is boring, the preaching is dreadful, and the people are somewhat irritating. I suppose you could add to the list.

But what I heard this week from my occasional attendee was this: "Preacher, I will be back to church one of these days, now that I'm caught up." You smile, shake hands, and depart with the feeling that somehow your presence made them feel awkward and uneasy. Why is it that people tell their preacher all of their assorted reasons for not doing what they know full well to do? Could it just be 'preacher conversation' that I should take with a grain of salt, or is there some underlying conviction they are saving their conscience or giving me permission to explore the issue more fully? I don't know. At any rate, I couldn't get away from his admission that church attendance would be brought back on the 'front burner' now that he is 'caught up'. Caught up?

There are times when the above statements are mine, too. Whether it is a day off, some needed rest, getting away from it all, finding some quiet place, being free of the routine and habit, or seeking more variety and diversity in my life.

I soon imagine the above reasons are not really addressed to me, but to God. For example, "God, Sunday is my day off..." or "God, I have been so busy I just haven't had the time, but I will be back, now that I am caught up."

And from a distant hill, you just might hear the muted sound of a broken heart, saying, "You've got a lot of catching up to do."

October 3, 2005

The Winning Ticket....

Last week's entry entitled, "I'm Caught Up" had to do with an individual who told me he'd be coming back to church soon because he was 'caught up'. Kind of like putting God 'on hold' because there were more important things to be done. Well, I had another doozy recently. A local businessman, after learning that I was a United Methodist minister, said, "I am Methodist. I don't go much because I am pretty busy. In fact, I guess I will just have to take my chances. That's the best any of us have anyway, right? A chance." Chances? "Oh, I give on occasion. I am good to my family. Treat everybody fairly. I am not too bad. Yes, I just have to take my chances." It sounded to me like 'divine lottery.' Buy a chance...odds are awful, but there is a 'chance' you might win. It's surprising how many people buy their lottery tickets with some illusive dreams of winning the jackpot. I left that brief encounter wondering if God were interested in that kind of scheme. We use the word 'chance' in various ways. An employer might say to the new employee, "I am going to take a chance on you." We say as we greet someone we haven't seen in a long time, "Chance meeting you here." Sometimes we hear, "It happened by chance." It conveys the meaning that something occurred unpredictably without discernible human intention. Yet here was a business man, well intentioned and adequately educated, staking his life and the life that was yet to come on 'the chance' that the Omnipotent One will make the kind of allowance that causes the one who purchases a lottery ticket feel sure he's holding the winning ticket, even though the odds are "ten million to one".

At the other end of the spectrum is an elderly, sainted parishioner, Gertrude James. Ninety-three years old. The cancer on her face has returned. I took her for her first two radiation treatments this week. And I asked her about how she's putting all of this together. In her own spirited and saucy way of putting things, she said, "Well, Pastor Chuck, let me be frank with you. I have had a good life. And I have faced every turn 'head on' with the calm assurance that it is all in God's hands. And I intend to take these 25 treatments just like I have taken care of these 93 years. One way or the other, God will take care of me." Still thinking of my encounter with the businessman, I asked Gertrude, "What if it were just the opposite, Gertrude? What if you just said, "I can handle this situation all by myself; I don't need God and anything else." She turned and stared at me as if she'd been hit with a rock. Without hesitation, she replied, "then I would be the greatest fool that ever lived. You just can't get from here to there without God." It sounded like the Psalmist who said as much: "The fool hath said in his heart, there is no God." And she said it again, "God will take care of things." I mentioned to her the song, "God will take care of you." And together, Gertrude and I sang that song..."Be not dismayed whate'er betide; God will take care of you. Beneath His wings of love abide; God will take care of you."

The future may not look all that bright for Gertrude...93 years and all; but that isn't what concerns her most. God is going to take care of it. She is going to 'head on down the road' and face it with the assurance that she is not playing roulette. She's taking no chances. No 'rolling the dice' for Gertrude. She is not going to play the fool. Life or death, one way or the other, she is holding the winning ticket.

October 16, 2005

Browse-Shopping

Jane and I love to eat out! The other evening on our way to 'fine dining' Jane asked if we could slip into the mall. On our Friday 'date night', I thought, why not? There is no need to hurry. A stop off at the mini-mall would be just fine. My immediate thought was that Jane needed something. Obliging, I parked the car, and on our way into the mall I inquired about what she was looking for. And Jane said, "Sometimes, you just need to go browse-shopping." Browse-shopping? "Yes, it is good to go shopping without a list in hand." I wanted a fuller explanation. She continued, "There are times when you realize you need something or want something and are not quite sure what it is until you see it. That's browse-shopping." My thinking is one ought to be pretty sure what they need. Once that is known, then you go shopping to meet that need. Jane worked hard at trying to convince me that browse-shopping was fundamental to happiness. Well, when she put it that way, I decided to give it a try. So we meandered around a couple of stores, looking for that which would bring us happiness. And believe it or not, we did find a few things that we needed. Browse-shopping and fine dining make a good evening.

For the past two weeks, that idea of 'browse-shopping' stayed with me. I tweaked it a bit and relabeled it for tonight's ramblings—"Church browse-shopping". Not necessarily church-hopping around, trying to find one that fits; but the coming to church, Sunday after Sunday, going through the motions, sitting quietly while watching and listening, no list in hand, no awareness of needs and wishes. When I think of browsing, I usually have no intention of buying anything and when the sales attendant asks, "May I help you?" I always say, "No, thank you. I am just looking around." And the clerk assures me that is fine and encourages me to take my time. "Just let me know if there is anything I can do to help you." Probably thinking if I hang around long enough, I just might find some 'happiness'. And you know, that person shows up every Sunday on just about every pew in the church. Not interested in being helped, just looking around. They have little desire to be accommodated. They just want to examine the goods; and after all, it is a good place to go and look. It becomes rather routine and eventually the routine becomes habitual. The habit of saying, "No thank you, I am just looking" becomes a pattern of resistance. There must be something very alluring about this kind of 'church browse-shopping' because they will be back next Sunday with no intention of purchase.

On the more positive side of this kind of 'church-browse shopping' is this: You just might not know what you need or desire until you see and hear it. You know you are on a quest. Some honestly seek but are not aware of that which would assuage the gnawing inside. They have a modicum of hope that this 'church browse-shopping' will help. And then it happens. There are some in this category who have had their lives radically changed because of what they saw and heard, even though they had no intention of its occurring. They came browsing and left believing. They came just to look around and found themselves 'found out'. They gave in to the Divine Purpose and ended up purchasing that for which they were looking all along. Jane was right: Sometimes you don't know what you want or need until you see it.

So, come next Sunday morning, I ought not be surprised that there will be 'browse-shoppers' there who have little or no interest in purchasing; they just want to look around or be looked at. Yet again, there will be others who are not resistant to purchase but are waiting to see and to hear that which will spark—"That's it". And Pastor Chuck, the sales clerk, will ask, "May I help you?" and I'd better be ready to deliver 'the goods'.

October 25, 2005

The Mystery of Prayer

Billy Barrow is one of the most warm-hearted persons you will ever meet. A lifelong member of the Mayodan United Methodist Church, along with his lovely wife, Annie Ruth, Billy is 'Brunswick Stew King of Rockingham County'. He is one of the most revered men in the Boy Scouts organization. He called my office today and wondered if I could 'carry him to the doctor'. Of course. Billy is one with a tender heart. He said he wanted to share something with me today. And on our way home from the doctor's office, I noticed a tear coming down his cheek. "What is it, Billy?" And then he told a story, a story, he said, very few have ever heard.

"October 25, 1945. That is when it happened. Sixty years ago, today. I was in the Navy, a signalman serving on the U.S. Raymond. The naval armada was already beached at Samar, poised for the Philippine invasion. Our naval battalion had finished night duty, guarding the river inlet to the island. It was about seven o'clock in the morning when we got word that the Japanese navy, some twenty miles away, had begun shelling our fleet. Our five-inch gunners were no match for their eighteen-inch guns. I heard it coming. Just a few yards away it hit one of our ships and immediately it was destroyed. The battle ensued for over two and a half hours. It looked hopeless. Had the Japanese kept coming we would have sustained incredible losses, but the invasion changed. Who knows. All of a sudden, the Japanese turned around and left. It was one of the mysterious quirks of war that is left unexplained.

"As best we could, we began hauling in survivors and preparing our dead comrades for burial at sea. In about an hour we heard an airplane coming in through the clouds above us. It was a kamikaze pilot heading towards us. Guns were fired at it and missed. It hit an artillery boat, which is nothing more than a floating ammunition depot. The bombs, the gas, the fuel exploded. I watched in horror as the flames and the dust engulfed the sea. Even the water looked like it was burning, too. In fifteen minutes, it was gone. Blown to bits. Nothing. In three and a half hours, we lost 1,850 comrades. I can still hear the sound of bodies hitting the water as they made their final resting place in the ocean. War officials credited the U.S. Raymond for turning the course of the war around that day. The invasion was on and you know the rest of the story.

"About three months later I received a letter from my saintly grandmother, Susan Jane Shropshire. In her letter she wrote that one night she felt a strong need to get out of bed and pray for me, knowing that I was in danger. She said she knelt by her bed and prayed for two and a half hours, went back to bed and couldn't sleep. About an hour later, she returned to her bedside and prayed for another hour. I took that letter to my superior and he was moved and surprised. My superior took the letter to the admiral and they began checking the dates and times, and discovered that Grandma Shropshire's prayers had corresponded exactly to the day and time of that bombardment. No one can convince me otherwise — I was saved that day by Grandma's prayers. I have always wondered about that, why I was spared and hundreds weren't. Grandma said she couldn't answer that but that she just felt a need to pray for her grandson who was in danger. And they say that there is no explanation why that giant Japanese gunner, the Yamato, turned around that day that changed the course of the war."

Coincidence? Maybe. Just one of those things? Perhaps. Leave it to mystery? Okay. One of the absurdities of war? Granted. But thank God for all those grandmothers and anyone else who knows when it is time to pray; let loose—and all hell shudders and heaven responds. Even right in the middle of a war! Thousands of miles away, out there in the midst of the carnage of humankind's most dastardly deeds, a young sailor named Billy looked around him and knew that it could be all over in a minute. Yet, sixty years later, with tears in his eyes, he tells his pastor this story. Grieved over his fallen friends still buried at sea to be sure; but thankful for whatever mercy it was that saved him that day and for the memory of a grandmother who wouldn't let him be without prayers.

Veterans' Day is coming up. About 1500 veterans of World War II die each day. They soon will all be gone. May we never forget their sacrifices. Thanks, Billy, for telling me this story. And thanks, too, Susan Jane Shropshire, for praying. Your prayers were not only answered that day, they still are being answered in the life and witness of your grandson, Billy.

November 21, 2005

Thanksgiving Revisited

Very few hands went up Sunday morning when I asked how many would be having Thanksgiving with their extended families. Work schedules, distance, and a variety of other reasons make it difficult to celebrate this season like it used to be, at least for me. It was never complicated years ago when we all went to Grandpa Geller's for Thanksgiving. It was never a subject brought up for discussion. It was assumed that Thanksgiving and the Geller gathering were synonymous.

It all happened in a tiny, two-room house with outside facilities. Grandma insisted that we all sit down at the table, or at least nearby. Of course, when thirty people gathered, everyone was nearby. Grandma's statement (which I thought was original with her) was, "There's always room for one more." When the food was about ready, Grandma would ask us boys to go down to the basement and bring up the lard cans and the wooden chairs. At their house, you had to go outside to get to the basement. We lugged those 2x10 planks upstairs along with the chairs and placed those boards over the lard cans for support. And we would cram onto those rough-hewn planks for a place at the table. Sometime during the process of the feasting, Grandma would have to have a picture. You always took pictures. It was kind of a sacred ritual for Grandma. And her fatalism would sometimes crop up and she'd say, "You know, we just might not all be here next year; you know, we might not be together like this again." That kind of thinking permeated the Geller understanding of life.

Well, we would gather together, bunched up and touching one another whether we minded or not. And it seemed like everybody was talking at the same time. Often there were a few tears, most often laughter. Departing, though, was a little more difficult. It took longer than usual. You had to hug everybody. Some of them you kissed. We would load up in the car and Grandma and Grandpa would stand there by the gate until we couldn't see them any more as the car drove away down that sandy lane. But it was the meal, the time of eating. It was special. The real treat was to listen to Grandpa grumble as he carved the turkey, loving every minute of it. At prayer time, it seemed like I was the designated 'pray-er' for the occasion. And anyone there would notice Grandma putting her net prayer bonnet on her head as we bowed and prayed.

We knew that we wouldn't see each other for another year unless someone died. And there was always someone to remind us of that eventuality. The older folk would go over last year's obituary, calling out all the deceased they knew and with each name there would be an anecdote or two. With the stories, we younger ones got connected with the deceased. We didn't know Cy Cudney very well, but when Dad would say, "I remember when Cy...." somehow the memory or the very mention of the name took on some added reverence for life. Then you'd hear something like this: "Well, you never know. It could happen anytime." Grandpa would snap his fingers and say, "Yeah, he went like that!" He could snap his fingers so that it sounded like the breaking of a limb off a tree. And to this day, whenever I hear someone snap fingers I am reminded of that subtle cue about the fleet-footedness of time.

Well, we can't go back to the Geller homestead anymore. They are not there. That original portrait of thirty has pretty well dwindled down. But, here on the eve of this another Thanksgiving, I am taken back there in my memories, with a grateful heart. Getting the chairs, the planks, the lard cans, and finding a place to sit down...Maybe that is what Thanksgiving is all about—finding a place to sit down. Whether it is on a weather-beaten plank with some Pilgrims and the Massasoit Indians, or in an Upper Room with 12, or with some 30 at the Gellers, Thanksgiving is about finding a place to sit down! Jesus said to those seated one day, "I'll not be here at the next Passover. Let's take a picture of it." And He broke bread and drank wine. And He gave thanks.

"Lord, help me to find my place at the table—my place to sit down."

January 29, 2006

Blooming

It has been a good day! I got another chance to say a word on behalf of the One who got me into this in the first place. Sunday mornings still have their haunting allure. I still get a 'kick' out of trying to make sense of it all. Karl Barth once told some preaching students, "what are you doing up there, preaching God's Word with your words? Don't you know that when you do that you are standing between heaven and hell? Between God's grace and human need? And that is a dangerous place to stand unprepared." In spite of that scary warning, I take my chances every Sunday, standing there on perilous terrain, offering hardly anything more than a "cup of water" in His name or throwing a small seed to the 'wind of chance' in hopes that it finds decent soil in which to bloom. I don't see much blooming these days.

Well, I take that back. This afternoon, I went with our youth and their leaders to visit a dozen of our members in the nursing home. The youth had been making small gifts—painted glass crosses to hang in their windows. I shall never forget the looks of the elderly; those lost in time and space, for a moment came back, accepted their gifts as if they had discovered a lost treasure. Their smiles were 'thanks' enough. They were so appreciative of our coming, especially the youth. Youth have a way, without saying very much, of being carriers of goodwill and warm-heartedness. It was a joy to watch them give gifts, to hear them sing "Jesus loves me", and to say the Lord's Prayer together. I was proud of our youth. I don't know how much this meant to them. I suspect that years down the road, they will remember more clearly what happened today and it'll make more sense, too. I wouldn't be surprised that out of this group of youth, an element of goodness and grace will be manifested in wonderful ways through their lives. And to the extent that happens, blooming did occur today. And I take 'heart'! And if I look a little more carefully, blooming just could be happening all over the place. Therefore, I will dare to stand between 'heaven and hell', getting a 'kick' out of watching where blooming just might take place.

February 27, 2006

A Couple Pots of Gold

Church membership can be so casual and routine! It is often looked upon as one of those rituals that come in the course of the pastoral duties; sometimes devoid of joy and excitement. Don't tell that to Betty Richardson and Velma Brame, the latest members to join the Mayodan United Methodist Church.

Betty has been battling cancer for over a year. About six months ago, I met her in the parking lot at the Mayodan Post Office. I had heard of her illness and introduced myself to her. I knew Clyde, her husband, by way of my many visits to the Airport Restaurant. We shook hands and she remarked that she had heard about me and asked an interest in my prayers. We prayed together in the parking lot and that was the beginning of a growing friendship. I met with her for prayer a few times in her home. Her physical condition had been deteriorating gradually and had taken a turn for the worse. One day she asked about church membership. She confessed that she believed in Christ as her Redeemer, but also felt that it would be important for her to belong to a church. "Would you like to join our church?" Because of her frail condition, with her immunity system seriously depleted, she was advised not to be around crowds for fear of infection. She wondered if she could become a member without attending. I said, "Of course, you can." Her face lit up with delight. "Really? That is so wonderful. That is good news." So we made arrangements for her to join the church the following Sunday, with Clyde and other members of the family to be present and to stand in for her. Anyone attending that service will not soon forget the passion, tears, and joy as we welcomed this new member into our fellowship. Over the next couple of weeks, I made follow up calls and visits about every other day. Two weeks ago, I called the family together to anoint her with oil. She told me that the end was near. This past week she felt well enough to leave the house for a ride, just to see her surroundings again. She was describing that trip to me and I asked her what she enjoyed most about what she saw. She replied, "The sunset. The sunset was so beautiful." I sensed she was saying *more* than what she was saying.

I have been pondering that episode while contemplating the end of my pastorate here. I suppose when you come to the end of something, even a pastoral tenure, you see things differently. You look and observe through a different set of lenses. You want to get your 'house in order' so that the transition will be smooth. You want to leave the place better than you found it with the unfinished work done. And while one could have hoped that the journey would be longer, it is nonetheless, a 'sunset' of sorts, a transition time.

I wouldn't want to take that 'sunset' away from Betty Richardson for a million dollars. And while our 'sunsets' differ greatly in degree, the song writer penned it: "Beyond the sunset, O blissful morning…" Blissful, not because of the departure, but because of what is up around the corner.

This past week, Velma joined the church. It was quite unique. I don't suppose this has happened very often in United Methodism—Velma is 96 years old. She even has a valid driver's license. I got acquainted with Velma through George and Ruby Goad. George and Ruby have been befriended Velma for 20 years, visiting her and assisting her in various ways. They have become 'soul friends'. George suggested I visit Velma and I did. A few weeks later, she wanted to talk to me about church membership. I had forgotten that conversation and George reminded me of that last Thursday. So, the two of us went to Velma's house and we talked about her joining the church. She confessed that she didn't get out much but she would do the best she could. She told me about her faith, her belief in Christ as per personal Savior. She grew up Presbyterian, but because of her fear of driving (even with her valid driver's license), she hadn't attended the Smyrna Church in years. "For all I know, they have probably taken my name off the roll." And that is right—they took her name 'off the roll'. But she was quick to add that going to heaven is more than having your name 'on the roll' with the Mayodan United Methodist Church, it is more about friendship evangelism. About George and Ruby's care and compassion for this widow, who has never had the blessing of children. We have become her new, extended family. And thanks to the quiet witness of the Goads, Velma joined this past Sunday.

As she made her way down the aisle with her walker, helped along by Ruby and George, along with about 20 others joining in, she made her profession of her faith. Normally, people don't say anything publicly at the joining, but Velma did. She said, "I was baptized at eleven but didn't know much about the Christian walk. When I was seventeen I made my profession of Christ as Lord. And for these past 80 years I have walked with God. Years ago, I prayed to God that he would not let my body outlive my mind. God has answered that prayer. I am happy today for all my friends and for my new family."

Velma's mind is as sharp as a tack! She knew what she was doing. She didn't have to do this, join the church, but she did—at 96, in her 'sunset years' still wishing to make a statement. When I asked why she wanted to do this, she said, "I believe Christians should belong to a church. It is a witness." While I agree with her, I sensed that she liked what she saw in George and Ruby. And this past Sunday, the fruits of their labors came to bloom.

Well, there you have it. The two newest members of our church. Both in 'sunsets'. Both ready! Both reminding me to take it a day at a time, to live life fully and every once in a while, take in a sunset. Don't be surprised by what you might find there. In my case, with Betty and Velma, I found real treasures. "Beyond the sunset, O blissful morning"—not because of the departure, but because of what is up around the corner. Thank God.

March 5, 2006

"Planting Things I Won't See Flower

This past week while sitting on the deck I noticed three daffodils blooming in the back yard. My first thought was "It's the warm weather and the early flowers are already blooming." On the other hand, these three flowers have never bloomed in the back yard in the four years I have been here. And, there was no apparent design in their placement. They looked like 'volunteers' that had no set design when they were first planted. Right there in the yard where the mower had kept the grass down, these three prodigal plants apparently took advantage of the warm weather and worked their way up through stubborn soil and greeted me with their early spring coat of yellow. I called for Jane and asked how they got there? They are bulb flowers and someone had to have planted them. It is highly unlikely that a mole found a bulb in the front yard and burrowed its way to the back and left it. Certainly, no bird had anything to do with it. Why? She said, "Well, they had to have been planted. Maybe years ago, someone may have had a flower garden. And they have been in a dormant season. The warm weather. No foot traffic in the area and the yard mowing is still a few weeks away; just maybe they made a hurried trip to the surface to give us a little bloom in the back yard. And they aren't doing anyone any good there so I am going to take them in the house." And she did.

As I write this, the little vase with its delightful contents sits before me, each daffodil tilting its head in my direction. They look happy. Contented. Delighted. I know for certain that the 'mother bulbs' have been waiting at least four years to come to bloom. For some strange reason—that is the way it is sometimes.

Several years ago, I served as a chaplain at the University of Kentucky Medical Center. I was visiting a lady dying of cancer. I had made several visits to her before. She knew she had just a few days to live. When I entered her room she was planting seeds in several paper cups. I watched her for a while. She took each seed and gently placed it in the fresh soil, pushed it down, and covered it up. She looked up at me and said, "Did you ever plant anything you knew you'd never see come to bloom? My favorite flowers are nasturtiums. The seedlings will be planted in my front yard, along with the other flowers. These will be the only nasturtiums in that garden, so when my family sees them they will remember me. You know, Chaplain, it is important to plant things you will never see come to bloom."

We usually plant things with the expectation of benefiting from their harvest or beauty. But she was right, there are many things we plant with no assurance at all that we will see them flower into life. I am having to think about this 'pastoring thing' in this regard. Four years ago when Jane and I came to Mayodan we weren't under contract that anything had to happen. We were given an opportunity and obligation to be faithful to God's calling and to love people, And leave the rest to God. Kind of like planting nasturtiums. Planting, I suppose, is my task; bringing seeds to flower, is God's.

Yes, in this tandem-team, some seeds will never come to bloom, at least not in my time slot at Mayodan. Those seeds will lie dormant, I hope in healthy soil, and one day, it will all come together. Someone will have a new insight for goodness. Another might see the 'light' in new and wonderful ways. Still another, while struggling to make sense of it all, will muster enough courage to say, "I am on the way." If any of this happens at all, it will be because of a <u>faith in the possibility</u> of 'planting things I won't see flower'.

Maybe I ought to go to the back yard tomorrow and stake out the birthplace of these daffodils, do a little cultivating and protection work so that the mower will have to make its way around my new-found flower bed. Come next spring, just maybe the bulbs will give birth again in the springtime and others will be thankful.

March 19, 2006

March 20, 1998

You ask anyone around Mayodan this question: "Where were you on March 20, 1998?" And they will be quick to tell you that this was the day a tornado destroyed the United Methodist Church, along with wreaking havoc on the entire surrounding territory and causing a death in Stoneville. Eight years later, Phoenix-like, the church has risen out of the ashes of its destruction. Shortly after I arrived here, someone down at Ann's Market said, "There must be something wrong down there…this is the second time that the church has been hit by a tornado." There are some people who need neat, tidy, small answers to every situation. They insist that it must be explained. So, when a church gets whacked a couple of times via storms, there are always those who will be ready and willing to tell you about the evil that must be lurking in the neighborhood.

This week, Connie Fox, our church's historian, alerted me to a web page that attempted to explain tragedy as "God's temper tantrum." It used the Mayodan United Methodist Church as evidence that God is not good, and Jesus Christ ought to be abandoned because of his dirty tricks. They used an ugly caricature of Jesus, saying, "I'll huff and I'll puff, and I'll blow your church down." Several destroyed churches are used as proof of an angry God and a compassionless Jesus. When you get to the picture, you see the congregation gathered on the Sunday following the destruction, having worship in the open air. The caption reads, "Destroyed twice by tornadoes, and they still don't get it."

Granted it was a tough time for the good people of Mayodan. It tested their fiber and resolve. There were those who fled in desperation, looking for a safer haven, but most stayed. Most were committed to rebuilding. None I have talked with ever hinted at the thought of an 'angry God' or a 'compassionless Christ'. On the contrary, the theological underpinnings of this church mock that atheistic web page, stating 'loud and clear' that the Church of Jesus will never be diminished by a tornado or any force of destruction. There has never been any wavering on the belief that the church is not 'bricks and mortar' but a living, dynamic building that is erected on the Christ, as St. Paul says in Ephesians, "…the Chief Cornerstone…." And as Will Willimon has said, "If that is not true, we might as well subdivide the property into malls and Gothic boutiques." So let the 'gates of hell' try to prevail and they are doomed to fail. Let the nay-sayers posit their arguments against a malevolent deity and they will gag on their very words.

The Church? What is it? It is a faith statement, one found in the parable of the vineyard, where the owner leased out his land and sent three servants to collect his share of the crops. Each was beaten and returned to the owner, empty-handed. Finally, the owner pondered sending his own son. Surely, he thought, they will listen to my son. No, they ended up killing the owner's son, speculating that now the inheritance would be theirs. When Jesus completed the telling, they asked him, "What does this mean?" And Jesus quoted from the Psalter, "The stone rejected by the builders has become the cornerstone." They got it! And they wanted him killed. It is always that way when you try to build something without due respect to the 'cornerstone'. It will all collapse. Crumble. Fade.

There were 135 people in church this morning, giving radiant witness to the 'Body of Christ' that is looking into the tomorrows with renewed vigor and resolve to be "the lively stones built upon the cornerstone" (I Peter 2:5-6).

Mr. and Mrs. Donny Martin joined the church this morning—two more people staking their lives on the claim that Jesus Christ is the 'Cornerstone' and they are prepared to risk it all, tornadoes included; that God is not angry nor is Jesus a fraud.

Whatever the future holds, whatever circumstances present themselves, and whatever evil lurks on the pathway, the Church of Jesus Christ will meet it on the corner and will offer hope and faith. Eight years ago, March 20, was a difficult day. But that small congregation, sitting amidst the ruins, could sing, "Oh, for a thousand tongues to sing my great Redeemer's praise, the glories of my God and King, the triumph of his grace." And they picked up the debris, piece by piece, cleared the land and put the pieces back together again, because they believed in a 'building not made with hands, eternal in the heavens'.

I suppose, in the years to come, every March 20, there will be a host of people who will remember and be thankful!

April 6, 2006

It's All in a Day's Work

Every minister has heard it at least once: "It sure must be nice to work just one day a week." Of course, most of them never show up on Sunday morning anyway, so how would they know? On occasion, I have invited them to follow me around any day they would wish. To date, I have had no takers. It is another one of those trite sayings that attempts to be humorous—that the pastor shows up on Sunday and preaches the sermon and picks up his check. No time clock to punch and you can manage your time as you please. People on the 'outside of it all' see an empty church most of the week and on Sunday see the parking lot filled with cars. So it looks like a once-a-week kind of a deal.

Not bad if you can get away with it! If only it were that simple.

I was thinking about this while returning from a hospital visit following supper. I asked myself, "Well, Chuck, what *did* you do today?" Nothing extraordinary; so I journaled it out in my mind on my way home.

1. On Thursday morning I had breakfast with four men from the Men's Bible Class: Norris Griffin, R.L. Blackard, Don Stillwell, and Sam Lloyd Atkins. We have been doing this for three years. And from those 365 years of accumulated wisdom, you'd be surprised what comes out of our conversations.
2. After an hour with the men, I rushed back to my office to continue work on Sunday's sermon. If I don't have a pretty good idea about the sermon by Thursday evening, I get homiletical heebie-jeebies.
3. I drove to the Baptist Hospital in Winston-Salem and had lunch with Libby Parrish and visited with her husband, Eddie, who has been battling cancer since the first of the year. What a blest two hours we had together.
4. I made a call on a new family who has been worshipping with us.
5. I stopped by the office to deal with a couple of phone calls from those needing assistance, plus a few others related to church business.
6. I had a quick supper with Jane and then went to Morehead Hospital, to visit with Frances Martin and family.

As I say, it was nothing out of the ordinary…the usual stuff in the makings of any pastor's day. I guess it would be nice to work just one day a week!

There are times when this pastoral business haunts me, when I wonder about this vocation. I am coming to the end of it after about 50 years of putting the hand to the plow and not looking back. About 60 years ago in a little Pilgrim Holiness Church, I made my first response to the call of God in my life.

It has been an incredible, meandering trail of ups and downs, in grace and out of it, and with some right and much wrong. I have labored, not in vain, but offered little more than adequacy and He has taken it and blessed it; and here and there, now and then, good has happened! And I wouldn't for a hundred worlds take any of it back. It's all in a day's work.

p 25 K of G comes at its best
87 Church holiness
forgetting our own history has a way of distorting truth
129 Prayers answered + still being answered in the life + witness of ─ church membership ─ witness to Christ

Hymn ─ God will take care of You
126 to God